THE JEWISH RESISTANCE

THE JEWISH RESISTANCE

UPRISINGS AGAINST THE NAZIS IN WORLD WAR II

PAUL ROLAND

This edition published in 2020 by Arcturus Publishing Limited
26/27 Bickels Yard, 151–153 Bermondsey Street,
London SE1 3HA

DA005602UK

Printed in the UK

MIX
Paper from
responsible sources
FSC® C018072

Contents

Introduction

THE MYTH

THIS ACCOUNT REVEALS THE EXTENT OF JEWISH resistance to the Nazis and their collaborators during the Second World War, and so dispels a popular misconception that the Jews went passively to their deaths in the Nazi extermination camps, led 'like lambs to the slaughter' from the ghettos to the gas chambers as so many accounts of the Holocaust would have it. That version of events is not only inaccurate but a pernicious myth which serves to exonerate those who stood idly by. They justified their failure to act by arguing that if the Jews did nothing to save themselves, why should they risk their lives to intervene?

And yet, according to Gideon Hausner, chief prosecutor at the Eichmann trial, there was 'much organized and widespread resistance', although it seems inconceivable that so many were able to fight back, and so effectively, when they were poorly armed, untrained and half-starved. However, it is a fact that in almost every ghetto and slave labour camp, and even in the concentration and extermination camps, there were organized Jewish groups who planned escapes, accumulated arms or made improvised weapons. Some carried out isolated acts of sabotage and the harassment of the enemy by any means they could contrive and at every opportunity.

But resistance to tyranny does not always involve violence or revolt. In such a brutal and pitiless environment, even the collection and distribution of extra food and essential supplies was an act of defiance. Small acts of kindness such as the sharing of their meagre rations took on great significance and strengthened the determination of the persecuted to endure their suffering and survive. Their one hope was to live to see their tormentors acknowledge their guilt and answer for their crimes.

When it was clear that the Allies would not bomb the railway lines leading to the death camps, nor the gas chambers, prisoners at Sobibór and Treblinka in Poland organized successful revolts, while at Auschwitz inmates sacrificed themselves to dynamite the crematorium. Their courageous acts were not intended primarily to avenge, but to save lives.

Beyond the barbed wire of the concentration camps, hundreds of Jews were active in the French underground and more were fighting with the partisans in other occupied countries, as well as those who had formed Jewish guerrilla groups after escaping from the ghettos. In the conquered countries of Eastern Europe, Jews held leadership positions in more than 200 partisan groups, but their true identity was only revealed decades later as these men and women had changed their names to avoid betrayal by their own comrades. A further one and a half million served in the Allied armed forces.

Those who could not arm themselves, or who were unable to fight back, contributed what they could. In the Warsaw ghetto, prior to the armed uprising, Jewish tailors sabotaged a consignment of German military uniforms by sewing the trouser legs together and stitching the buttons on backwards, knowing full well that their actions would cause nothing but annoyance and that the repercussions would be terrible. But even such ultimately futile acts were preferable to doing nothing, to submitting to enslavement. If they were to die, they would die with dignity, as human beings and not as subhumans (*Untermenschen*) – a category into which they had been placed by their would-be Aryan masters.

Guerrilla units

Many of the stories contained in the following pages only came to light recently, uncovered in the archives of Jewish cultural institutions in the Eastern Bloc following the fall of the Soviet Union. Other accounts had originally been published in Yiddish and Hebrew by the participants themselves or by surviving witnesses, and so were not consulted by non-Jewish-speaking historians. Instead, the latter relied largely on historical reports and official accounts filed by the Germans, which gave a false impression of the extent and intensity of the resistance offered by their inadequately armed opponents.

In drawing upon these previously neglected sources, this book reveals how thousands evaded the brutal round-ups and trans-portations to form themselves into well-organized guerrilla units, surviving for months, even years, in the forests and mountains where they lived off the land, their wits, their courage and, occasionally, sheer luck.

Without Allied assistance and with little hope of living long enough to see their liberation, these vastly outnumbered bands of untrained insurgents frequently proved themselves as formidable and resourceful a force as the partisans and under-ground resistance groups who were sponsored and supplied by the Allies. But although free, they faced more fearful odds than their compatriots – for they fought not only the Nazis but their own countrymen, collaborators and all the virulent anti-Semites who would have turned them in, or killed them on sight.

Chapter One

A QUESTION OF FAITH

THE JEWS HAVE ALWAYS LIVED IN HOPE, sustained by their faith and strong family ties as well as a deep-rooted sense of tradition, which has enabled them to endure exclusion, persecution and the pogroms to which they were periodically subjected.

Such experiences, together with their fervent belief that they would one day find a safe haven from their enemies, instilled in the Jewish psyche a sense of fatalism and a dogged determination to survive, despite all that they had suffered.

And so, when the Nazis seized power in Germany on 30 January 1933, the Jews of Europe were in the main anxious rather than fearful. Many of them expected that the new government would soon fall prey to the inter-factional fighting that had brought down previous administrations, necessitating yet another of the fiercely fought elections which had become a recurrent feature of the Weimar Republic. There was no reason to assume that they had seen the last of these until Hitler sought 'emergency powers' through the Enabling Act on 23 March. This gave the regime the authority to pass laws without the approval of the Reichstag, which legitimized Hitler's dictatorship and put an end to democracy in Germany for the next 12 years.

The Nazi race laws became increasingly draconian as the administration drip-fed the population with pernicious anti-Semitic propaganda in order to pursue its long-term aim of ridding the Reich of 'the enemy within', namely the Jews on whom they blamed all their ills – chief among which was the nation's humiliating defeat in November 1918.

The fact that 100,000 Jews had served in the German army during World War I and that 12,000 had died fighting for the Fatherland counted for nothing with the National Socialist government. Initially, there were grudging concessions for Jewish veterans, due in no small measure to the protests of President von Hindenburg, who declared that anyone good enough to fight and die for Germany should be honoured regardless of his race. But after his death in August 1934, the Nazis ramped up their racist campaign, prohibiting the names of the Jewish war dead from appearing on public memorials and insisting that Jewish veterans were removed from the membership lists of ex-servicemen's associations. Jews, said Nazi Propaganda Minister Joseph Goebbels, were not Aryans and therefore not true Germans.

And still the Jews of Germany clung on to the vain hope that the Nazis' anti-Semitic rhetoric would moderate once the regime had flexed its muscles and won all the territorial concessions that Hitler was to acquire by bluff, bullying and brinkmanship.

They told themselves that the iniquitous laws denying them basic civil rights, prohibiting them from public places and barring them from the professions (the so-called Nuremberg Laws of 1935) would be repealed in the wake of international condemnation. But the European democracies and the United States voiced little more than muted disapproval, for fear of becoming embroiled in a second costly global conflict. Both expressed their sympathy for the plight of German Jews, while submitting to Hitler's increasingly outrageous territorial demands in the vain hope of delaying the inevitable. It could and has been argued that non-intervention allowed the Allies more time to rearm, but at the time they were seen to have sacrificed the Jews of Europe along with the non-German-speaking inhabitants of the Rhineland, the Sudetenland and Czechoslovakia, in order to pacify a dictator and placate the pro-fascist lobby and the appeasers.

Jew-baiting

When the former Bavarian corporal annexed his motherland of Austria in March 1938, a wave of anti-Semitic persecution erupted on the streets of Vienna that was said to have surprised even the Nazi leadership. Evidently the regime's anti-Semitic measures had gained popular and widespread support within the Reich.

That autumn all German and Austrian Jews were forced to surrender their passports, which were stamped with a red letter 'J' so that the holder could be readily identified. The more affluent among them were blackmailed into paying an extortionate emigration tax before being allowed to leave the country. Many had their passports confiscated to prevent them from emigrating and among those who remained anxiety now gave way to apprehension.

A few weeks later, on the night of 9 November, their fears proved to be well founded as a supposedly 'spontaneous' yet clearly co-ordinated campaign of Jew-baiting broke out across Germany and Austria. This was in retaliation for the assassination in Paris of a German diplomat, who had been shot by a young Polish Jew. On the night that was to become known as *Kristallnacht* (the Night of Broken Glass), thousands of Jewish-owned businesses were attacked by mobs of brown-shirted paramilitary SA Stormtroopers. More than a thousand synagogues were desecrated and set alight and Jewish homes were ransacked and their occupants beaten and terrorized by Nazi thugs. Hundreds of Jews were murdered in the days and weeks that followed and a further 30,000 Jewish men were sent to concentration camps.

Kristallnacht was hotly condemned by the foreign press, who could no longer avert their eyes from the open hostility being shown towards Jews in Nazi Germany. The London *Times* reported: 'No foreign propagandist bent upon blackening Germany before the world could outdo the tale of burnings and beatings, of blackguardly assaults on defenceless and innocent people, which disgraced that country yesterday.'

Goebbels revelled in the destruction that he had initiated until Hitler raged that Germany could no longer claim that the stories of Jewish persecution were unfounded slurs perpetuated

Kristallnacht, or the 'Night of Broken Glass', was a pogrom led by SA paramilitaries throughout Nazi Germany. The windows of Jewish-owned businesses and buildings were smashed at the same time as synagogues were destroyed.

by the 'Zionist press'. National Socialism had long been accused by its enemies of being a brutal totalitarian regime and now it had finally been exposed as such. Hermann Goering too was incandescent with rage, blaming Goebbels for ordering the wanton destruction of property and businesses that the regime could have confiscated and sold on to its supporters. It was only when Hitler promised to levy a one billion mark fine on the Jews to cover the cost of the clean-up that the smirk returned to Goering's face, as he enjoyed the cruel irony of it all.

Prior to *Kristallnacht*, German and Austrian Jews had had their citizenship revoked, their civil rights rescinded and their freedom of movement restricted. Even their children were prey to pernicious discrimination, having been expelled from state schools to ease 'overcrowding'. Before that, they had endured years of being verbally abused by both their classmates and their teachers, who routinely held Jewish pupils up to public ridicule and refused to intervene when they were bullied by other students. And still there were many in the Jewish community who persisted in the stubborn belief that they were witnessing just another outbreak of rabid anti-Semitism and that the storm would pass.

At the mercy of the Nazis

But after *Kristallnacht* the Nazis intensified their hounding of the Jews by instigating a succession of measures that moved inexorably towards their eventual elimination. A central office for emigration was established to 'encourage' wealthy Jews to leave, provided that they signed over their property and valuable possessions to the Nazi authorities.

Those who could not afford to pay, or who were unwilling to hand over all that they had worked for, were deprived of contact with the outside world with the confiscation of their wireless sets and telephones, as well as being forbidden to use public calling facilities.

A curfew was also introduced, which made them virtual prisoners in their own homes. And in 1939 one of the last in a series of almost 2,000 anti-Semitic decrees legitimized the eviction of Jews from their places of residence without notice or a reason being given.

If any still retained hope that they might be spared a worse fate than had befallen the Jews of 15th century Spain or 19th century Tsarist Russia, they were soon cruelly disillusioned. On 1 September 1939, German troops invaded Poland, leaving its European allies, who declared war on Germany later that day, with no time to concern themselves over the fate of the Jews inside the Reich. By June the following year France and the Low Countries were under Nazi occupation after a lightning victory had subdued Germany's old enemies in just six weeks. The British were forced to evacuate their shell-shocked troops from Dunkirk, abandoning their heavy weapons and vehicles on the beaches.

Suddenly all the Jews in Europe were at the mercy of one of the most murderous regimes of modern times, for out of the many brutal dictatorships who left their bloody mark on the 20th century the Nazis alone planned the systematic extermination of an entire race, utilizing an industrial method of genocide. And it was this method of mass murder that ensured that the victims did not resist. They simply had no idea that such a fate awaited them.

Those who feared the worst were torn between resignation and suicide, an act prohibited by Talmudic law. It has been estimated that more than 3,000 chose to die by their own hand in Germany alone rather than face deportation to the camps, a figure that can be radically increased when those who committed suicide in the wake of the Nazi boycott of Jewish businesses and *Kristallnacht* are added. By the spring of 1942, the Jewish population of Germany had been reduced from 575,000 to just 132,000 and only a tiny proportion had managed to emigrate. The Jews of Eastern Europe would have no opportunity to flee.

The Wannsee Conference

The Nazis wasted no time in herding the Jewish population of Poland into ghettos, with the first (Piotrków) being established just eight weeks after the invasion. The following month, Jews from Austria and Czechoslovakia were deported to Poland, marking the first stage on the road to Auschwitz and the other extermination camps. In total, 11 extermination camps were built between May 1940 and July 1942, with a further 15,000 detention and slave labour camps being constructed in the occupied countries.

Polish intellectuals and political leaders were among the first to be liquidated in May 1940, in mass executions carried out by the *Einsatzgruppen* (the SS paramilitary murder squads charged with 'ethnic cleansing' in Eastern Europe) and their Soviet allies, while the Jews were isolated until their fate could be decided.

At this time, there was no plan to exterminate the Jews en masse. No Führer decrees had been issued, or at least none have survived. Hitler was in the habit of expressing his desires in an impulsive and casual manner, which his functionaries would turn into written and detailed directives, thereby absolving him of responsibility and leaving him free to blame his subordinates if they failed.

It seems likely that the original intention to forcibly deport all Jews from the Reich evolved into a detailed plan to exterminate all of the Jews in Europe sometime in July 1941. This was when Goering authorized Himmler's deputy, SS Obergruppenführer Reinhard Heydrich, to implement what the Reichsmarschall termed 'the Final Solution to the Jewish Question'.

The practical considerations of this 'project' were discussed

Reinhard Heydrich was one of the architects of the Holocaust. He chaired the Wannsee Conference in 1942, which formalized plans for the Final Solution.

with chilling clinical detachment by senior Nazi officials at the Wannsee Conference in Berlin on 20 January 1942, over which the icily efficient Heydrich presided.

Before this time, mass executions of Jews were perpetrated at random by the *Einsatzgruppen*, who followed in the wake of the Wehrmacht and the SS as they cut a swathe through Poland. As each town and village was overrun, the Jews were rounded up and taken to a secluded spot where they were shot and their bodies dumped in freshly dug pits. News of these atrocities only became known because they had been committed with the complicity of locals, who would boast of their part in eradicating the Jews from their region. But it was initially received with scepticism by Jews and Gentiles alike, who saw it as no more than an alarmist rumour or anti-Nazi propaganda, just like the stories of the death factories and the slave labour camps where men, women and children were starved, brutalized and worked to death.

Consequently, when in 1941 the Germans informed Jewish leaders in Poland, Ukraine and the other occupied territories that the inhabitants of the ghettos were to be 'resettled' further east, the operation was organized with the reluctant co-operation of the *Judenrats* (Jewish councils). It was enforced by the Jewish voluntary police, who saw to the orderly evacuation of the civilian population.

The Judenrat

The role of the *Judenrat* in the Holocaust has been the subject of heated debate and controversy, with writer Hannah Arendt asserting that they played an active part in the round-up and transportations by compiling lists of Jews and their property as well as authorizing the Jewish police to enforce Nazi orders. That may well be true, but certainly their compliance must have proved an additional deterrent to those Jews who were considering offering more than passive resistance.

For their part, the Germans were confident that the Jews would not resist. The majority were women, children and the elderly, while the men and youths were unarmed, untrained and had no access to weapons. Besides, they would not put their families at risk by taking up arms against the German military, who had made it clear that any acts of resistance would meet with bloody and indiscriminate reprisals.

It was not until the autumn and winter of 1942 that the population of the Warsaw ghetto discovered the true destination of the transports, from one of their number who had been assigned to follow the trains to Treblinka. At the same time word of the atrocities being perpetrated by the Nazis reached the outside world through a Polish resistance officer, although the Allies subsequently offered no assistance to the Jews who remained imprisoned in the ghetto and in the camps.

From January 1943, the Jews of Warsaw were certain that the next round-up was imminent and that it would be the last. They knew that they would be fighting for their lives and that they would have to fight alone. Even the Polish underground initially refused to help them until they saw how fiercely they fought with what little they had.

That spring, the Germans learned to their cost how ferociously the Jews could fight when faced with annihilation. For 14 weeks several hundred beleaguered inhabitants of the Warsaw ghetto fended off thousands of crack SS troops with little more than handguns and home-made bombs. Even the Nazi propaganda machine could not silence the news of their courageous stand, nor of the aftermath which saw the levelling of the ghetto and the transportation of the survivors to the death camps. A total of 55,000 Jewish men, women and children were taken away, according to official German sources.

Murder, Inc.

In all, the Nazis had planned to exterminate an estimated 11 million people after evacuating all of the Jews from Western and Eastern Europe by a combination of force and deception. The idea appealed to the neat, orderly mind of the Nazi bureaucrats and functionaries who had devised the plan at Wannsee. Men such as SS Obersturmbannführer Adolf Eichmann.

It was Eichmann who would co-ordinate the transportation of the two million Jews murdered at Auschwitz and boast of doing so. He had once taken one of his mistresses on a 'working holiday' to Hungary, where he personally supervised the rounding up and deportation of Jews to Dachau and Auschwitz. He informed the lines of huddled and frightened people that Auschwitz was a 'holiday camp' and that only married couples were eligible to enter, so those who were still single should get married if they wanted to be allowed inside. His cynicism knew no limits. He had even written postcards on behalf of his victims, urging their relatives to waste no time in coming out to join them.

Eichmann had learned basic Hebrew in order to ingratiate himself with the leaders of the community and convince them that not all Nazis were as bad as they had been painted. It was a typically duplicitous ploy and one in which he evidently took a sadistic delight. He also took pleasure in coining some of the terms with which the Nazis endeavoured to conceal the true nature of their crimes. As masters of what would become known as Orwellian doublespeak, they spoke of taking victims into 'protective custody' and offering the Jews 'special treatment'. Eichmann later confessed to having enjoyed his 'work' and was proud of having been an efficient administrator, though he denied being the architect of the Final Solution. That 'honour', he insisted, belonged to Heydrich. He admitted to being criticized only once by his superiors, when he had ordered twice as many people as usual to be crammed into the cattle trucks. His defence was that many were children, and so wouldn't take up as much space as adults.

But as he was a compulsive liar and fantasist who was bent on making his own part more significant than it was, it is hard to know if he was telling the truth when he claimed to have dictated the letter of 31 July 1941 on behalf of Goering, ordering Heydrich to implement the Final Solution. Nor is it known if he was merely boasting when he claimed to have persuaded his superiors to adopt the use of the pesticide Zyklon-B instead of carbon monoxide to speed up the extermination process. The only statement that can be taken at face value is the one he made while on trial for his life in 1962, when he regretted that he had not murdered more Jews.

'We didn't do our job properly. We could have done more. I didn't just take orders. If I had been that kind of person, I would have been a fool. Instead, I was part of the thinking process. I was an idealist.'

In a world where such men had been given the power of life and death, there was no alternative but resistance.

Chapter Two

IN THE LION'S DEN

A shot in the dark

As the son of a rabbi, David Frankfurter grew up with a strong sense of tradition and knowledge of the Torah, which contains the core teachings at the heart of Judaism. He was also familiar with the Talmud, the collection of rabbinic discourses on the meaning and interpretation of Jewish law as it had been entrusted to Moses by God. From his earliest years in Hebrew 'class', David had been taught to obey the 13th commandment – 'Thou Shalt Not Kill' – which stated that the shedding of blood (*shefikhut damim*) is the primeval sin (Genesis 4:8). But he was also aware of the Old Testament proverb 'an eye for an eye' and of the impassioned debate among biblical scholars about whether this saying permitted the taking of the life of another to obtain justice or revenge. He wrestled with this distinction in 1936, after hearing the Swiss Nazi leader Wilhelm Gustloff inciting extreme nationalists to call for the adoption of Hitler's anti-Semitic decrees in a country which valued its neutrality.

David had emigrated from Germany to Bern two years earlier to continue his medical studies after he had been prohibited from attending Frankfurt University because of anti-Semitic Nazi laws. He was alarmed to see that the cancer of Nazism had taken root among German-speaking Swiss nationals and was desperate to do something to draw attention to the threat it posed to the country's Jewish community.

He found little sympathy for his concerns among his fellow students and there was no condemnation of Gustloff's racist rants in the Swiss press. Out of a mixture of concern and curiosity he attended a Nazi rally and heard for himself the racist speeches that called for the extermination of the Jews.

The publication of the notorious anti-Semitic forgery *The Protocols of the Elders of Zion* and the subsequent court case in Bern in May 1935 – which saw it condemned by the judge as a work composed of 'forgeries, plagiarism and obscene literature', but which also gave the defendants a public platform for their anti-Semitic slurs – only aroused Frankfurter's ire and convinced him to take action. He had originally planned to assassinate another Nazi Party leader, but abandoned his plan when he thought he had been

David Frankfurter (left) had a strong religious upbringing. He wrestled with his conscience before deciding to take action against the Nazis.

discovered. Then he seriously considered assassinating Hitler, but feared that such an action would have horrific repercussions for all Jews in Germany. Switzerland's own would-be Führer appeared to be a much easier target.

On the snowy morning of 4 February 1936 the 27-year-old student bought a revolver and travelled to the town of Davos, where he found the address of Gustloff's second-floor apartment in the telephone directory. After being admitted by Gustloff's wife he went into his office, which was furnished with Hitler mementos, and shot him three times. A fourth bullet went wide of his target. He then went to a neighbouring apartment from where he telephoned the police and calmly confessed to the murder.

The Nazis portrayed Gustloff as a martyr and made much anti-Semitic propaganda out of this one isolated act, but the regime decided that they could not afford to use the assassination as a pretext for widespread violent persecution of the country's Jews in case it jeopardized attendance at the Winter and Summer Olympics, which were both to be staged in Germany that year.

The Swiss subsequently prosecuted Frankfurter and sentenced him to 18 years in prison. His conviction was quashed in June 1945, but the Swiss insisted that his release did not negate his guilt and ordered him to pay restitution and the prosecution costs.

During his incarceration, his distraught father (who was to die in a Slavonian concentration camp with three other members of his family) visited his son and demanded to know how he could justify what he had done. David's answer is not recorded, but his son Moshe is certain that the assassination was justified.

'It kept the Nazis out of Switzerland, and the lives of 20,000 Jews who lived in Switzerland were safe,' he said. It was an act of self-defence, one could argue, not murder. Moshe added: 'From a historical point of view, was the assassination justified? My answer is very clear.'

The great deception

The Nazi state was built on violence and sustained by terror and intimidation. Fear was its most effective weapon.

The fear of starvation and the promise of 'work and bread' had convinced many of the unemployed and underprivileged to vote for the National Socialists during the economic crisis of 1929, while the better off were persuaded by the party's promise to tear up the hated Versailles Treaty and reject its punitive reparations bill. As Hitler's popularity gathered momentum in the early 1930s, it was the fear of not belonging and of being seen as insignificant that drove many to join a party that appeared to promote unqualified and unprincipled petty functionaries to positions of influence and power over their fellow citizens.

After Hitler's accession to the Chancellorship in January 1933 and the passing of the Enabling Act in March which effectively legalized the dictatorship, it was the fear of informers and the dreaded Gestapo that silenced those who might have spoken out against the regime's pitiless repression of free speech and its persecution of the Jews and other minorities. And it was the fear of the outsider, mixed with innate suspicion and ignorance, that persuaded Germans and Austrians to support the Nazis' racial policies, which excluded Jews from public life, as much as the insidious propaganda that fed their bigotry and belief that they were the Master Race with a divine right to rule and enslave their supposed 'inferiors'.

It is almost impossible for the citizens of a totalitarian state to depose a tyrant unless there is a widespread popular movement galvanized by an irrepressible desire for change and even then a popular revolution or coup is unlikely to succeed without the support of the military. There was no such desire within Nazi Germany in the early years of Hitler's reign. Quite the contrary. After the bloodless seizure of the French-occupied Rhineland on 7 March 1936, the assimilation of the Führer's home country, Austria, on 12 March 1938 and the 'reclaiming' of the Sudetenland by 10 October that year, Hitler was hailed as a second Bismarck, the man predestined to restore Germany to greatness following its humiliating defeat in the First World War.

Germany's influential foreign 'friends' voiced their grudging respect for the former corporal's audacious statesmanship, while even the most cautious of Germany's citizens were caught up in the euphoria which swept through the much-enlarged Reich. It was only after Hitler had devoured Czechoslovakia with the shameful collusion of the Allies before invading Poland on 1 September 1939 that his most vociferous critics were finally shown to have been right. Hitler had desired war from the start. His volatile and turbulent nature craved it and his belligerent vindictiveness against the world at large had only intensified with each concession granted him by the war-weary appeasers.

With the blitzkrieg victories of May 1940, Hitler's popularity with the German people was at a peak. He was omnipotent and irreproachable in their eyes. This being the case, the armed forces dared not stage a coup for fear of being seen as traitors. Even if they had, it was unlikely that the ordinary German soldier would have obeyed them for Hitler had shrewdly and cynically commanded them to take an oath of allegiance (the *Reichswehreid*) to him personally as their Führer on 2 August 1934, which their soldier's code of honour forbade them to break.

Only those with nothing to lose could risk sacrificing themselves to defy such a regime.

Jewish youth fight back

In Germany, long before the outbreak of war, clandestine Jewish cultural organizations had been formed to provide work for Jews who had been dismissed from their jobs and official posts in the wake of anti-Semitic Nazi laws. Temporary schools provided work for unemployed teachers and education for pupils prohibited from attending the state schools. As the Nazis tightened their stranglehold on power, Jewish groups and individuals engaged in subversive activities in order to maintain a semblance of normality, despite the increased surveillance and the risk of being reported by informers.

Thousands fled from Hitler's Reich, leaving friends, family, property and possessions behind for a new life in America and other neutral countries, in itself a courageous act. Those who risked their lives to facilitate their escape or who provided false papers, sanctuary and other assistance for the Jews who chose to remain in Germany and Austria defied the dictatorship at the risk of their lives and those of their friends and families. On the other hand, many of those who complied with Nazi edicts to wear the yellow star did so either because they lacked the means or the strength to fight back, or because they simply could not envisage the fate the regime had planned for them.

While their elders stubbornly clung on to vain hopes or succumbed to despair, some of Germany's Jewish young people were determined to act, despite a lack of weapons and training. A small number organized isolated attempts on the lives of Nazi officials, but without arms, training or support the majority of Jewish youth groups were limited to printing and distributing leaflets, monitoring foreign radio broadcasts and providing aid to the remnants of demoralized, but defiant anti-fascist organizations. These were made up of communists, socialists, intellectuals, students, union leaders and Christian activists, who opposed the dictatorship on moral grounds. The scale of resistance activities can be gauged by the fact that 32,500 trials were held between 1933 and 1944 for acts of treason against the state and the death sentence was imposed in all cases.

The Baum group

Of all the accounts recording Jewish resistance to Nazi tyranny, the least well known and arguably the most remarkable are those detailing the activities of the Baum group, for this group of young idealists operated in the heart of Germany – Berlin. In

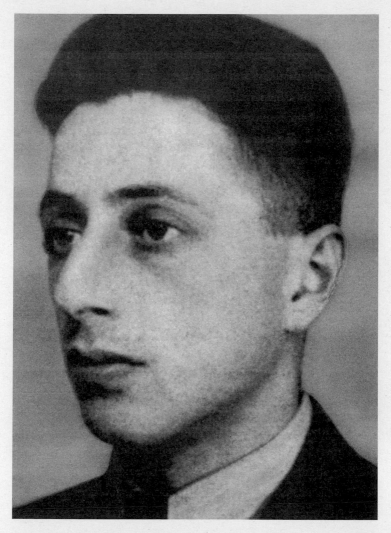

Left-wing Jewish activist Herbert Baum who was tortured to death by the Nazis in Moabit prison, Berlin on 11 June 1942.

1941, the year they embarked on a campaign of active resistance to the regime, the average age of its members was just 22.

The majority of the group had been recruited in 1938 by the young anti-fascist activist Herbert Baum from among the 1,000 Jewish slave workers labouring under armed guard in the Siemens factory in Berlin. As Jews, they were obliged to wear a yellow Star of David on their clothing to identify themselves. To remove it was a crime punishable by death and yet they risked such a penalty in order to move freely in the city and make contact with other resistance groups, all of whom were reluctant to work with the Jews because of the extra risk this entailed. However, the group's isolation ensured its security. There were no outsiders who might be persuaded to betray them and their shared faith and culture bound them together as closely as if they were a family. Herbert and co-leader Martin Kochmann had also been close friends since childhood and there were several couples among the other members.

At first they were content to meet socially in an effort to continue to live as normal a life as they could under the circumstances, but inevitably the discussion would gravitate towards the possibility of demonstrating their hatred for Hitler and his gang. Then in 1941 they learned of a Jewish resistance group in Buchenwald concentration camp. It was headed by Rudi Arndt, who had organized the sabotage of various SS activities inside the camp. Arndt was subsequently murdered by the *Sicherheitsdienst* or Security Service (SD), but details of his activities were circulated by a former inmate who had managed to escape and these had inspired other groups to emulate Arndt's successes.

Herbert Baum decided that a public demonstration in honour of Rudi Arndt was called for at the Weissensee Jewish cemetery, the second-largest Jewish cemetery in Europe. The ceremony attracted a sizeable gathering of supporters and emboldened the group, who then began printing and distributing anti-Nazi leaflets among the Siemens workforce, as well as posting them to private homes and business premises and putting them up in public places. They were aided by two non-Jews: a German office worker and a French typist, who made stencils in their own homes for printing the pamphlets. For a year, the group were able to put up their posters and paint anti-fascist slogans in prominent places with little fear of discovery.

But they also provided a focus for serious political debate in the private homes of members and sympathizers, which enlarged their sphere of influence. In addition, they organized educational events to keep the community well informed, which was essential at a time when access to the foreign press and listening to Allied radio broadcasts was forbidden. Ironically, the only serious opposition they encountered during two years of intense militant activity came from a rival Jewish organization in Berlin. This group considered it more important and more urgent to use their limited funds and resources to help Jews to escape by providing forged passports and temporary shelter until they could be smuggled out of the country.

But this must have given Herbert Baum the impetus to procure forged documents from the foreign civilian slave workers who had been taken from France, Holland and Belgium. These were issued to members of the group so they could continue their work outside the city. Funds for this were obtained from membership fees and then through audacious thefts of valuable paintings from the homes of wealthy Jews in a suburb of Berlin, whom Baum and his accomplices conned by impersonating officers of the Kripo (Kriminal Polizei). The money was also used to fund the group's future activities and the purchase of food to supplement the meagre rations of Jewish slave workers.

Had they restricted themselves to such activities they might have continued to be a thorn in the side of the regime while accumulating considerable funds to buy forged documents to help their fellow Jews flee the country. Tragically, they decided to risk everything on what amounted to a futile symbolic gesture – the destruction of an anti-Soviet exhibition which had been opened to much publicity on 8 May 1942 in the Lustgarten in the centre of the city, off the Unter den Linden.

Tragic anti-Nazi gesture

Das Soviet Paradis (The Soviet Paradise) had been the idea of Dr Joseph Goebbels, the Propaganda Minister, known to comrades and enemies alike as the Poison Dwarf because of his diminutive stature and acid tongue. The title of the exhibition was characteristic of Goebbels' biting sarcasm and was intended to reveal the 'poverty, misery, depravity, hunger and need' imposed on the Russian people by the 'Jewish-Bolshevik' communist system and the imminent threat to the Reich posed by the Soviet advance.

Anti-fascist cells in Berlin such as the Schulze-Boysen-Harnack group were determined to expose the real purpose of the exhibition – to divert attention from recent German defeats in Russia – by posting leaflets and bills all over the city. But the Baum group saw it as their chance to let the world know that a Jewish resistance cell was active in the heart of Hitler's empire.

The destruction of the exhibition would be a significant blow to Goebbels' prestige and could be carried out with minimal risk to the group. They were also encouraged by the assurance that another anti-fascist cell, the Franke group, would be able to supply them with a sufficient quantity of explosives and inflammable compounds, as its leader worked at the Berlin Chemical Institute.

By Sunday 17 May, more than a million people had visited the exhibition, so there was every reason to expect that the operation would ensure considerable publicity for their cause. After reconnoitring the site, it was agreed that an arson attack would have a good chance of success, but that it should take place at noon the next day as there would be fewer visitors on a weekday and so less chance of a bystander intervening.

Unfortunately, although the operation was carried out without a hitch, the fire was quickly extinguished and the damage was minimized. As soon as he heard about it, Goebbels gave orders that the story was to be suppressed so nothing about the incident appeared in the press.

Predictably it gave the Gestapo a pretext to arrest and torture suspected members of the underground and any Jews that they had under surveillance – as if they needed one. Within a week all of the leaders of the Baum group, along with their friends and associates, were brought into Gestapo headquarters, which led some to wonder if an informer had betrayed them. But it is more likely that their inexperience had left them vulnerable. They had trusted too many people and been too open in expressing their anti-Nazi views. Members of the Franke group were also seized and subjected to interrogation.

More than 500 Berlin Jews were arrested, though few had been politically active in any capacity. Two hundred and fifty of these were shot as 'terrorists' and the remainder transported to Sachsenhausen concentration camp. Their families were interred at Theresienstadt in Czechoslovakia. Herbert Baum was beaten to death in his cell by the Gestapo without revealing a single name to his assailants, but his friends could not afford to take chances. Braver men and women had been broken by the Gestapo.

Fearing that the arrests and executions were only the beginning of a crackdown on illegal groups, the surviving members of the Baum group destroyed all the literature and other evidence that might incriminate them and dispersed to lodgings in the suburbs, using their forged papers.

They were kept informed of the Gestapo investigation by the nurses in the Jewish hospital where Baum founder member Sala Kochmann had been taken after she had attempted to escape by jumping from a window at the police headquarters. She had been afraid of cracking under torture and so had tried to kill herself, but she only succeeded in breaking her spine. She thus endured indescribable agony until the day she was executed.

Nazi justice

The sham trials to which members of the Baum and Franke groups were subjected disclosed the true nature of Nazi 'justice'. The proceedings of the Sondergericht (Special Court) were held in secret and the accused were refused the right to be defended by lawyers of their choice or to call witnesses in their defence. The verdicts were made public through placards posted around the city, on which the middle names of all of the accused were shown as 'Israel' or 'Sarah', implying that only Jews opposed the dictatorship. As the Polish Holocaust historian Bernard Mark observed, the trials of non-Jewish German anti-fascists were generally not publicized.

All of the accused members of the Baum group were found guilty and all but three of these were sentenced to death, the youngest being just 19. The sole surviving member of the group, Richard Holzer, escaped to Hungary. The three female members who were spared the death penalty – Alice Hirsch (20), Lotte Rotholz (20) and Edith Fraenkel (21) – were transported to Auschwitz, where they perished. Two other female members who had been sentenced to death were subsequently reprieved. In all, 22 members of the Baum group were executed. The Nazis were particularly brutal in their treatment of their victims. They chose to revive the barbaric tortures and executions of the Middle Ages by beheading them with an axe or the guillotine, including the women.

The descriptions of the executions are too distressing to recount here and it raises the question of whether it would have been better for the group members to have put all their ingenuity, courage and energy into evading detection in order to outlive their persecutors. In that way they could have served as witnesses instead of sacrificing themselves in a symbolic gesture that seemingly had so little effect.

Communist heroes

In 1981 the German Democratic Republic (GDR) finally recognized the sacrifice made by the young Berliners by erecting a small monument in the Lustgarten. Characteristically, it made no mention of the fact that almost every member of the Baum group was Jewish, only that they were communists opposed to the fascist regime.

A few blocks north-east of Berliner Allee in former East Germany is Herbert-Baum-Strasse, which the GDR named in honour of a committed communist who gave his life attempting to sabotage a Nazi exhibition maligning the Soviet Union.

As writer David Michael observed in his revealing survey of anti-Nazi monuments in Berlin (for the website Humanity in Action), the memorial to Baum is dwarfed by that commemorating the Aryan wives of Rosenstrasse, who took to the streets to protest against the deportation of their Jewish husbands in February and March 1943 and succeeded in forcing Goebbels to release them.

Equally deplorable is the scant mention of Jewish resistance in the German Resistance Memorial Centre in Stauffenbergstrasse, on the former site of the Reichswehr headquarters where Colonel Claus von Stauffenberg co-ordinated the failed plot to assassinate Hitler in July 1944. Only one of the 26 sections in the Memorial Centre records the efforts of the Berlin Jews, though the Baum group is mentioned specifically, as well as those who took part in the ghetto uprisings and the revolts in the extermination camps. It also mentions the Jewish Kulturbund, which organized cultural and sports events for Jews who were banned from participating in public events under Nazi laws.

However, there is no acknowledgement of the Zionist underground youth group Chug Chaluzi (Pioneer Circle) which was active in Berlin and which supplied forged documents, shelter and food to Jews in hiding until they could be smuggled out of the country. Nor of its counterpart, the Community for Peace and Reconstruction founded by Werner Scharff and Hans Winkler, which operated in the suburbs of Berlin from June 1943 until October 1944.

David Michael notes that the official guidebook is almost

The Otto Weidt Museum in Berlin is one of the few sites in modern Germany to commemorate the Jewish resistance.

exclusively devoted to the failed attempts by factions within the German armed forces to depose Hitler and his henchmen. It gives the impression that the blame for the murder of millions of people, the destruction of German cities and the division of post-war Germany should be attributed solely to the Nazi leadership and not the German military or the population, who were so vociferous in their support of the dictatorship.

The celebration of the courage shown by individual Berliners such as Otto Weidt, who employed blind and deaf German Jews in his workshop, appears to be an attempt to assuage the collective guilt of those who failed to act and those who chose passive opposition (or 'internal emigration') and to explain the 'temporary insanity' of those who supported the regime only because they had been enthralled by a malevolent mesmerist. This is a defence that does not stand up to scrutiny.

Chapter Three

RESISTING THE INVADERS

Resistance in the occupied countries took many forms other than armed struggle. Under the noses of Nazi officials thousands of Jews were smuggled out of Nazi-occupied countries by organized cells and courageous individuals, in defiance of the edicts which forbade anyone to aid or assist Jews in eluding their fate. Other acts of rebellion included the publication of underground newspapers, the performance of plays, the organizing of poetry recitals, concerts and art exhibitions and even the solitary act of keeping a diary. All of these were prohibited acts punishable by death, but they were carried out regardless in order to foster solidarity and sustain morale.

In Western Europe, there were no ghettos and few laws restricting the movement of Jews. Consequently, European Jews made up a significant proportion of the membership of urban and rural guerrilla groups in France, Italy, Belgium and Greece, although they constituted a tiny percentage of the population.

Belgium

As early as September 1939, the Jews of Belgium anticipated an inevitable German invasion by forming what is believed to have been the first Jewish resistance group outside the Reich. Many of them (between 80 and 90 per cent) were refugees from Eastern Europe and were acutely aware of the threat posed by the Nazis. As the German blitzkrieg rolled over Belgium's ineffective defences in May 1940, they joined the exodus of civilians choking the roads to southern France. Their perilous journey was made all the more hazardous by German Stuka dive-bombers, which machine-gunned the refugees to spread panic and impede the retreating Belgian army.

But after the fall of France on 22 June, many made the arduous journey back to Belgium to avoid internment by the Vichy government, which controlled France's non-occupied zone. It was a prudent decision, for many of the thousands of Belgian Jews who remained under the 'protection' of Marshal Pétain's puppet government were subsequently transported to Auschwitz along with the French Jews.

At first, the returnees were not subjected to overt persecution by the German occupation forces, but they knew it would only be a matter of weeks or months before the round-ups began. However, the Germans were in no hurry. Hitler may have been an impulsive, indolent and irrational personality, but his functionaries were methodical, meticulous and fastidious to the point of obsession. They wanted to be sure that not a single Jew would evade their net.

The first stage of their insidious master plan required the isolation of the Jews from public life. In October 1940, the first anti-Jewish decree was issued in Belgium, which required all Jews to register with the Belgian authorities and have 'Jude' (Jew) stamped on their identification cards. It was swiftly followed by the compulsory registration of Jewish businesses, which the owners were forbidden from selling to anyone other than the occupation authorities, who offered no more than a token payment to provide the appearance of legitimacy.

The following year, Belgian businessmen were compelled to deposit their capital in a central Nazi-controlled bank and to comply with an order that gave German officials the right to monitor all transactions and productivity, an edict which made them the servants of their Aryan overseers.

In 1941 Belgian Jews were also excluded from education and the legal and medical professions and were barred from working for the press and the radio.

Although the Nazis did not establish ghettos in Western Europe, they confined the Jewish inhabitants to specific cities and districts within those cities. In Belgium these districts were created in Brussels, Antwerp, Liège and Charleroi, where a curfew served to keep the Jewish inhabitants together in readiness for the deportations. A *Judenrat* was established in November 1941, which lent the appearance of legitimacy to the round-ups, giving the impression that these had been endorsed by the community elders.

The Germans accumulated information for almost two years, amassing files in anticipation of the order to implement what they euphemistically called 'the Final Solution to the Jewish Question'. This followed the Wannsee Conference of 20 January 1942, when senior Nazi officials and representatives of the SS drew up plans for the systematic extermination of Europe's Jews. By July, the deportations had begun.

The hiatus also gave the Nazis' intended victims time to organize clandestine links to the supply of financial aid to Jews who were in hiding and false papers for the thousands who wished to flee to neutral countries. But among the young in particular there was a fierce resolve to defy the oppressors in any way they could. In Belgium, these militant-minded men and women joined the active Zionist organizations Solidarité and Fraternal Aid, which advocated armed resistance as the only practical means of self-defence.

Solidarité also published an eponymous paper in Yiddish in which they called on their fellow Jews to refuse to work for the Germans, as even the making of clothes for the Wehrmacht assisted the enemy. They also warned of the implications of co-operating with the Association des Juifs en Belgique, as the Belgian *Judenrat* was called, and they carried out isolated acts of sabotage including the mining of German supply trains and the selective assassination of collaborators. Among these was one of their own associates, who had been assisting the Germans with drawing up lists of Jews for deportation.

Opposing the Judenrat

Opposing the edicts and influence of the *Judenrat* proved to be as challenging as any military operation, as the partisans had to convince their own people to defy the Jewish council. In July 1942, when the first of the deportations began, the *Judenrat* called on the community to comply with the order issued by the German authorities, which required them to appear at the assembly points for resettlement in work camps to the east. Many believed that the work camps would be their final destination or disregarded the advice of the underground for fear that their families would also be deported if they failed to appear. With time against them, the commanders of the three units in Brussels were forced to approve a raid on the *Judenrat* offices where the files were kept, in order to prevent these from being handed over to the Gestapo.

The *Judenrat* office was in a busy district of the city opposite a building used by the Wehrmacht and the raid had to be undertaken in daylight as the first deportation was to take place the following day.

Two Jewish partisans bluffed their way into the building by pretending to be from the Gestapo. They then held the staff at gunpoint while two accomplices who had followed them inside scattered the files on the floor and doused them in petrol, before setting them alight. Once the fire had taken hold, the four men slipped out and melted into the crowd on the busy Boulevard du Midi.

The raid convinced some of the *Judenrat* staff to resign, but the deportations resumed the following month. No fewer than 10,000 Jews were transported to Auschwitz, necessitating a second attack on the collaborators. On this occasion one of the most prominent members of the Jewish council in Brussels was assassinated in broad daylight in the hope of demonstrating that no traitor was safe. And still the deportations continued, while the Gestapo redoubled its efforts to find the 'Jewish bandits'.

Following an extensive and brutal round-up of Jews in Brussels in September 1942, the country's Jewish leaders considered the rescue of what remained of the country's 90,000 Jews to be a priority. It was imperative that a network of safe hideouts should be found, especially for the children.

This became the responsibility of the CJD (Committee for Jewish Defence), which organized sanctuary for them in children's homes and with Belgian families with the connivance of the Church and charity organizations. By these means, the CJD saved 3,000 Jewish children and facilitated the safe passage of 10,000 adults into neutral countries. Some of these children were the offspring of Belgian Jewish partisans, who were then free to join the fight without the added anxiety of worrying what was happening to their families. The CJD also provided an underground infrastructure for Jews fleeing persecution, which was unique to Belgium.

The country's Jewish leaders recognized the necessity for a legitimate representative organization that could act as an intermediary between their community and the general population. There was also a need to lobby certain institutions and influential individuals who might be willing to speak on behalf of the Jews and provide financial aid for both its official and clandestine activities.

Belgian partisans

By the spring of 1942, there were three units of Jewish partisans operating in Belgium. Each comprised just three men, to reduce the risk of detection and minimize the loss if they were captured. For greater security each operated independently and was kept in the dark regarding the identity and location of the other units. But within a year the support network had swelled to 70, with resources including a rudimentary laboratory for manufacturing explosives and printing false documents. In addition to these units there were dozens of Jews fighting in guerrilla groups in the Low Countries which had no Jewish affiliation.

The links established between Jewish and non-Jewish groups proved vital when they needed to pool information or launch a combined operation, as happened on 19 April 1943.

That day news of a train carrying 1,500 Belgian Jews to Auschwitz reached the Jewish defence committee only hours before the deportation began.

Fortunately they were able to co-ordinate an attack with the help of a group led by George and Alexander Lifshitz. The brothers were familiar with the route the train would have to take and they knew of a place where it could be stopped, a remote rural location at Tirlemont in Flanders.

As the train approached, George flagged it down and then the partisans scrambled aboard and broke open the cattle wagons, freeing their human cargo. As many as 700 men, women and children jumped down and ran for cover as the German guards opened fire, killing 20 and wounding another 10. The elderly and those who were unlucky were soon recaptured, leaving more than 300 to seek shelter in the forest and the surrounding countryside.

Eight of the wounded were taken to Tirlemont Hospital, from which they were rescued on 2 May by the partisans. In a daring assault, they surprised the guards and bundled the wounded into three vehicles, which then sped off into the night.

The Germans had as a matter of routine placed roadblocks on strategic sections of the main road into Brussels and the convoy found their escape route obstructed by armed German police. As the first car accelerated into the barrier, the two passengers emptied their machine guns into the Germans, who scattered. The two rear vehicles carrying the wounded veered down the side roads. All returned safely to the city.

Holland

When the Dutch government surrendered on 15 May 1940 after the bombing of Rotterdam, the entire Jewish population of the Netherlands – some 140,000 people – found themselves at the mercy of Hitler's executioners – the SS and the Gestapo. Only

30,000 of Holland's Jews managed to evade capture and transportation to Auschwitz or Sobibór, many of them finding shelter with sympathetic friends and neighbours. These 'righteous Gentiles', who were honoured after the war by Yad Vashem, were more prevalent in the Netherlands than in any other country, reinforcing the impression that the Dutch were an exceptionally tolerant nation, liberal-minded by nature and predominantly fiercely anti-extremist.

When the Germans attempted to impose their propaganda in the form of state-sponsored films and newsreels the Dutch audience booed or walked out en masse. Tens of thousands defied the decree prohibiting them from listening to broadcasts by the BBC and the Dutch government in exile. Passive resistance was endemic and demonstrated itself in a series of national strikes in 1941, 1943 and 1944. It also took the form of seemingly innocuous acts such as placing a postage stamp on the upper left side of the envelope to signify that the sender reserved the upper right corner for a stamp bearing the face of their queen, Wilhelmina.

The Dutch were slow to offer active and violent resistance, being a law-abiding nation by tradition. However, a groundswell of resentment and open defiance began to gather momentum once the Germans imposed severe restrictions on their freedom of movement and demonstrated their brutality in putting down the February strikes of 1941. These had been organized by the outlawed Dutch Communist Party. This bitterness intensified with the forced conscription of Dutch labour into Germany in 1943, inducing even the most compliant citizen to support the

Dutch resistance fighters in Breda, the Netherlands in 1944 after liberation. They are carrying weapons taken from the Germans.

activities of the Dutch underground, in spirit if not in action. That year 85 per cent of Dutch students refused to sign an oath of loyalty to their new German masters.

It has been estimated that 50–60,000 people were actively involved in the Dutch underground, which provided a network of support for those in hiding in the form of false papers, money and food. Ten thousand of them paid for their defiance and selfless actions with their lives.

But it was impossible to save all of Holland's Jews. A total of 107,000 were rounded up and transported, of whom only 5,000 survived to return at the war's end. There were only 18 survivors from the 34,000 transported to Sobibór. In all, three-quarters of Holland's Jews were exterminated.

The biggest contributing factor to this catastrophic loss was the fact that Holland offered no means of escape. It was bordered by countries under German occupation and its North Sea coast was patrolled by German vessels. Many more Jews might have been saved had they not refused help for fear of endangering their hosts and their own families, who would have been left behind. Almost all of those who were offered shelter were individuals, though Anne Frank and her family were an exception. It was simply too dangerous to shelter entire families in the face of the ever-present threat of routine house-to-house searches and the risk of discovery by informers.

The flat featureless terrain offered few hiding places, yet Dutch Jews risked arrest and torture by the Gestapo by joining the resistance. Their activities included attacking prisons and liberating the inmates, destroying registration facilities and files and assassinating collaborators.

Greece and Italy

In Greece and Italy, Jews and Gentiles fought side by side rather than form separate groups, taking advantage of the rugged terrain to stage lightning attacks before melting back into the mountains. After the German invasion of Greece in April 1941, the Jews of Salonika and Athens joined the two national resistance groups, the National Liberation Front and the National Popular Liberation Army, while more than 1,000 Italian Jews swelled the ranks of the Garibaldi group and the Freedom and Justice Fighters.

As the total number of Italian partisans is believed to have been between 6,000 and 7,000, this represents a significant proportion. And of these, a sizeable number were women. Contrary to the popular image of the typical young resistance fighter, there were many older men in the movement – some of them veterans of the Great War, whose experience proved valuable – and boys as young as 13. According to Jewish tradition, a boy becomes a man at the age of 13, and so the Jewish resistance saw nothing wrong in allowing boys to join the fight. The youngest fatality in Italy among the Jewish partisans was 13-year-old Franco Cesana.

Over the course of the war 100 Italian Jews were killed in fierce fighting with Mussolini's Fascists and their German allies, while others were tortured to death or executed after their arrest.

The partisans lived in fear of their lives 24 hours a day, unsure of whom they could trust. As well as risking their lives in combat they were also continually waging a war against privation and the elements. With no uniform to identify them, they were not treated as prisoners of war by the Germans, but as 'bandits' and were summarily shot or tortured.

The Germans frequently ignored the Geneva Convention when it came to their treatment of partisan prisoners. In one case, that of Eugenio Calò, they buried him alive when he refused to divulge the names of his comrades under torture.

The courage, loyalty and endurance of these inexperienced fighters is all the more remarkable when one recalls that they were not professional soldiers, or men and women who had received any formal military training. They were shopkeepers, manual workers, doctors, teachers, artists and students.

To single anyone out as remarkable would be a disservice to those who remain largely anonymous, but Mario Yacchia, a founding member of Freedom and Justice and a leader of the partisans in Emilia, is worthy of special mention. His group were surrounded in a house in Parma after they had been betrayed by an informer, but Yacchia remained behind to destroy important documents while the others made their escape. After he was captured, he was tortured but he could not be broken and was executed. His selfless courage was recognized after the war by the Italian Republic, which awarded him the golden medal for bravery.

The same medal was posthumously awarded to Rita Rosani,

the only woman to die in battle. The 23-year-old teacher had been a founder member of the 'Eagle' group and was killed in Verona, where a street has been named in her memory.

Italian Jews played a vital role in facilitating communications between the advancing Allied armies and the French Maquis and were active in assisting Allied prisoners of war to escape from Italian prison camps. Silvia Elfer and her brother Eugenio supplied thousands of escaped Allied prisoners of war with food, medicine and essential supplies in their makeshift camp in the Abruzzi mountains. Her brother was executed by the Germans but Silvia was accidently shot and killed by an American GI.

Not all of the Jewish partisans were willing or able to take an active part in the fighting, so they contributed what they could to the struggle. The underground radio network and the free press were crucial elements in maintaining the flow of information, news and anti-Fascist propaganda. A former literary critic, Leone Ginzberg, was important in the underground printing network in Rome. He was arrested and died under torture and is the only Jewish partisan to have a street in Rome named in his honour.

Of the 45,000 Jews living in Italy before the war, 6,000 emigrated following Mussolini's adoption of anti-Jewish decrees and 10,000 were deported to concentration camps.

France

French Jews constituted the vast majority of the membership of both the First and Second Detachment of the Communist FTP-MOI (Francs-Tireurs et Partisans–Main d'Oeuvre Immigré) and also formed all-Jewish units known collectively as the Armée Juive, which originated with Zionist youth groups in Toulouse in January 1942. Although many of the Jewish resistance fighters

French Jews in a detention centre near Paris from which they were deported to the extermination camps, July 1942.

were committed Zionists (who hoped to establish a Jewish homeland in what was then Palestine), the majority made it clear that they were fighting for France and for their heritage. Armée Juive chief Jacque Lazarus declared: 'Hunted as Jews, we wanted to show the enemy that it was as Jews we fought.'

Although primarily an active military force, the Armée Juive also organized the safe evacuation of hundreds of Jews to Spain and Switzerland.

In the summer of 1944, following the D-Day landings, a number of small underground units joined forces and formed a new fighting group to harass the retreating Wehrmacht. They called themselves the Organization Juive de Combat and were active in the liberation of Paris and other major French cities in August of that year. But their most audacious operation saw them capturing a German troop and ammunition train wearing Star of David armbands and taunting their prisoners with the cry '*Ich bin Jude!*'

Identifying the Jews

While the French Resistance and their rural counterparts in the Maquis fought to liberate France from German occupation, the members of the Jewish Partisan Unit of Paris were driven by a more immediate concern – to protect themselves and their families from transportation to the Nazi extermination camps.

The majority of its members had emigrated from central and Eastern Europe, where they had been subjected to persecution by their own countrymen. Many had brought their wives and children with them in the belief that they would find work and a better quality of life in France. But with the swift victory of the German Wehrmacht in June 1940, and France's subsequent capitulation, they found themselves trapped in occupied territory. They had no choice but to lie low in the hope of evading the round-ups that would see their compatriots transported to Auschwitz with the collusion of the despised Vichy government.

The Germans assumed that the French would oppose any orders issued by the occupation authorities, but believed they would obey instructions issued by their own government, albeit a puppet administration who were regarded by their compatriots as no better than collaborators.

The occupying force soon identified which Vichy ministers they could count on to implement their plans to rid France of its Jews, as there were several vociferous anti-Semites only too willing to serve their Nazi masters. However, the problem they faced was that the French authorities had no way of identifying their intended victims as the last French census had taken place in 1874. So the Germans established the General Commissariat for Jewish Affairs and its subsidiary the General Association of French Jews to collate all information that might be useful as a first step towards segregation.

With the exception of the recent immigrants who crowded into the densely populated 11th arrondissement (administrative district) of Paris on the right bank of the Seine, French Jews did not tend to congregate in specific districts. Nor did they identify themselves unless they were orthodox and therefore in the habit of wearing the traditional clothing required by their religion. The majority of the country's Jewish population had successfully assimilated, but they knew it was only a matter of time before they were discovered and subjected to the 'special treatment' meted out to their fellow Jews in Germany, Austria and Poland.

The German authorities were aware of the difficulties they would face in identifying the Jews, and so they deliberately delayed implementing anti-Jewish measures. They did so in the belief that those who had fled into the Vichy region and into the suburbs and villages of the occupied zone might be lured back to their homes and businesses if given sufficient time to persuade themselves that it was safe to return.

By the autumn of 1940, the occupation authorities had exhausted their patience.

Role of the French police

Under a Vichy decree issued on 4 October 1940, all Jewish refugees were stripped of their civil rights and were subject to arrest by the French police. In addition, all Jews in the occupied zone were required to register with the French police, who stamped their documents 'Juif' (Jew). The German and Polish émigrés knew from experience that this was only the first stage in isolating them from the general population, so they ignored the summons. But the French Jews were on the whole more trusting and they obeyed the order.

A total of 40,000 French Jews from both zones were subsequently interred in transit camps in Paris under the watchful eye of armed French police, together with 30,000 German Jews who were forcibly deported to the capital later that month.

The following spring, on 13 May 1941, the Germans ordered all foreign Jews to report to their local police station, together with their families. They were told to bring sufficient food and clothing to last them for two days and were informed that they were to be 'resettled' in the east, although in truth they were transported to the internment camps and thence to extermination camps. Five thousand Jews dutifully obeyed the order.

In August the first of the periodic round-ups began when a further 5,000 were forcibly evicted from their homes and crowded into cattle wagons bound for Auschwitz. Many died en route from thirst and malnutrition. Those who survived the journey were killed in the gas chambers within an hour of their arrival.

Despite the willing and occasionally openly enthusiastic participation of some Vichy ministers, who initiated the additional round-up of children that their German masters had not even required, only a fifth of France's 300,000 Jews were deported. This was thanks partly to local officials who resented being used as pawns by their 'old enemy' and who regarded their victims primarily as French citizens and therefore not subject to Nazi race laws.

Although anti-Semitism existed in France, as it did everywhere else, the French had an innate hatred of 'the Boche' which outweighed any suspicion that some might have harboured towards the Jews in their midst. Consequently, the Germans could not count on their co-operation as they would do in Poland – quite the opposite in fact.

Partly as a result of this reluctance on the part of the French police and officials to co-operate with Vichy, 70 per cent of French Jews survived the Holocaust, compared with only 10 per cent of the Jews in Poland. Less than a tenth of those Jews who were deported from France were French nationals. The remainder were stateless and had been dependent on the charity or protection of wealthier Jews who had fled the German advance. They therefore had no one to intervene on their behalf. That said, the assistance offered by the French police resulted in the extermination of 120,000 French Jews, 25,000 of whom were children.

Vel' d'Hiv

Each time the French police were ordered to assist their Nazi overseers they were informed that the operation was necessary to eradicate 'foreign spies'. However, no such lie could have fooled the French gendarmes into believing that they were doing their patriotic duty after the Vel' d'Hiv raid of 16–17 July 1942.

Over the course of those two days 30,000 Jewish men, women and children were rounded up and corralled inside the Vélodrome d'Hiver, a glass-domed sports stadium near the Eiffel Tower. They were held under police guard and were denied food, drink and even basic sanitation. The only water to drink came from a single tap, the lavatories had been locked and all windows had been screwed shut to prevent anyone from escaping. As a result, the heat generated by the glass roof was stifling.

Despite protests by the Red Cross, the Vichy minister in charge declared that the conditions were 'satisfactory' and barred doctors from attending to the sick. A number were driven by desperation to escape and were shot while several committed suicide in full view of the others.

Some of the French police must have been sickened by these scenes and the sight of so many fragile and malnourished people in such obvious distress, but they were being closely observed by the Gestapo and were under strict orders from their superiors.

The Vel' d'Hiv round-up remains one of the most shameful

On 16 and 17 July 1942, more than 30,000 Jews were rounded up and held in terrible conditions inside the Vélodrome d'Hiver in Paris.

episodes in French history and one which tightened the resolve of the Jewish Partisan Unit of Paris to intensify its harassment of the hated occupying forces.

Diary of a Parisian partisan

Abraham Lissner was a Polish émigré who went to France in 1929 and was a veteran of the Spanish Civil War, where he fought against Franco's fascists as a member of the Jewish partisans known as the Botwin Company. After his return to France he became a leader of the Jewish Partisan Unit of Paris.

On 15 March 1942, Lissner took the unusual and hazardous

step of keeping a journal of his activities and the comrades that he fought with. That night a mutual friend acting as an intermediary brought Lissner a message inviting him to meet a young Jew named Sevek Kirschenbaum, who wished to discuss 'an important matter'. Three days later Kirschenbaum and Lissner defied the 8 pm curfew to discuss the practicalities of forming a Jewish Partisan Unit in Paris. They had both come to the conclusion that the distribution of pamphlets was not enough and that only an armed struggle could defeat what Kirschenbaum called 'the modern cannibals'.

Some days later Kirschenbaum arranged for Lissner to meet a fellow Pole, Leon Pakin, who had also served in the Botwin Company in Spain and who convinced Lissner that the core of the new unit should be organized around ex-members of that Jewish guerrilla group. There were other Jewish groups in France fighting the Nazis, but they were isolated and their operations were unco-ordinated.

Lissner's entry for 27 April recorded the first setback before their operations had even begun. Two members of the group tasked with making a bomb to be planted outside a German barracks were injured when it exploded prematurely, one of them fatally. Worse was to come as no fewer than 17 of their comrades were arrested when they went to the hotel where the bombers had been staying, unaware that the mission had been compromised.

Two weeks later the group steeled themselves to threaten the life of one of their own who had been accused of doing business with the Germans. With few weapons at his disposal, Lissner was forced to carry a toy pistol with which he terrorized the man before taking his money, which they donated to the cause.

FTP resistance organization

At this time they possessed a few revolvers which they had acquired from another Parisian resistance group, who informed them that none of the units in the city had sufficient weapons. Later they would be supplied by the Allies, but in the early months of the occupation they were reliant on their own resources and ingenuity.

However, by June they were under the command of the FTP (Francs-Tireurs et Partisans), the national resistance organization which would co-ordinate the operations of the various units and supply them with weapons and explosives. Lissner's group was one of four operating in Paris, the others being an Italian group, an Armenian group and a Romanian group which also included Hungarians. It was believed that each of them would be more effective and less vulnerable to betrayal if they could remain independent from the other units, and so they were composed exclusively of their own countrymen.

FTP Central Command would allocate missions according to the individual strengths of the four units, but the leaders of each unit would decide which members should be assigned specific tasks. Each unit had a courier to convey messages and reports to and from the central command. These were invariably women, who also had the dangerous task of carrying weapons and explosives across the city.

Members of the Francs-Tireurs et Partisans joined ranks with American paratroopers during the Battle of Normandy, 1944.

To avoid further accidents all bombs were assembled at one secure location, but then they had to be taken to the group that had been assigned the task of planting them. This was done at great personal risk by the women, who also had the responsibility of providing basic supplies and food and ration cards to the group, as it was easier for them to move freely in the streets during daytime. There was less risk of a woman arousing suspicion or being questioned.

One in ten lived a double life, working during the day and acting as partisans at night. It was considered too dangerous to do otherwise, particularly as the chance discovery of one could lead to the capture and execution of the whole group.

Recruitment

Recruitment was another concern. As desperate as they were to increase their activities, they had to be extremely cautious when it came to accepting new members as the Gestapo were continually attempting to infiltrate the underground. For that reason, every unit assigned one member to maintain contact with all anti-fascist organizations and exchange information regarding potential recruits. Frequently a new volunteer would claim to have been working with another group, and so it was vital that these claims be substantiated. Even staunchly loyal resistance fighters could be turned informer by the Germans if they had been broken through torture, or if they believed that their families would be shot if they did not co-operate. For that reason they were required to sever all links to their friends and family and find new lodgings, which they would rent under a false name.

It was important to establish a regular routine so as not to arouse suspicion. Every weekday morning they would leave at the same hour as if for work and return at a regular time. Without a job they would have to live on the 1,600 francs a month that the FTP would pay them. A married man with a child would receive 300 francs more a month, but family men were in the minority. However, if they had particular skills, connections or access to something the group needed then they might be admitted and in certain circumstances their family might be seen as good 'cover' for their illegal activities.

They could be under surveillance 24 hours a day and not be

aware of it, as the Gestapo would assign as many as 25 men to shadow a single partisan and they would not arrest them until they made contact with their leader. The Gestapo were tireless in their hunt for saboteurs and had the resources of the Nazi terror apparatus behind them, while the partisans lived on their wits and were all under the strain of imminent discovery. An anxious look or a moment's indecision could give them away.

Women as partisans

At 11 pm on an August evening in 1942, only minutes after planting a time bomb in the rue Pierre-1er-de-Serbie, Lissner found himself under the watchful eye of a German naval officer as the pair stood in a Metro station awaiting their train. They were the only passengers on the platform. Lissner's partners had been fortunate. They had caught their train in the opposite direction and made their escape. However, Lissner's train was late. Moments later came a deafening explosion. The station master shouted something and a policeman blew his whistle, but the German officer was slow to react and before the policeman could reach their side of the station, Lissner's train arrived and he was away.

The following month three women of the Jewish Partisan Unit in Paris were caught quite by chance in a routine police check and found to be carrying grenades. One was taken to her home, where the police expected to find an armaments cache. While they were searching her apartment, she threw herself from a window rather than be tortured by the Gestapo and was killed.

Her two companions were transported to Auschwitz where they presumably perished, as they were never heard of again.

Like so many of their comrades, the courage and sacrifice of these three women went unnoticed and unacknowledged, but some of the activities of the Jewish partisans did receive wider attention. That November, a bomb attack on a Montmartre hotel frequented by German officers was reported by the BBC and Radio Moscow, encouraging those who had taken part in the operation and those Parisians for whom such news provided a boost to morale.

Lissner's diary entries record two further bomb attacks in which German troops were killed – one on a military barracks on the rue de Vaugirard and the other in a location near the Place de la Concorde, where German soldiers were known to congregate. In neither case does Lissner speak of reprisals, although the Germans would not have allowed such 'outrages' to go unpunished.

Betrayed by a comrade

But by the spring of 1943 a number of key personnel from the Jewish unit had been killed in attacks or captured and executed. The partisan general staff believed that it was only a matter of days before the Gestapo located their hideouts, and so the decision was taken to disband the unit and for its members to scatter to the suburbs and shelter in the outlying farms. By June they were all active again, but were fighting with other units.

The pages of Lissner's diary for the rest of that year record missions in which his former Jewish comrades took part, most notably the assassination of Dr Karl Ritter, the Gauleiter (or Nazi district leader) responsible for the deportation of hundreds of thousands of Frenchmen to German slave labour camps.

Lissner admitted in his diary to a feeling of pride in having made a 'modest contribution' to the struggle to liberate Paris. From March 1942 to the winter of 1943, he kept a tally of successful hit and run attacks by both his own group and what he called their immigrant allies. These included 29 bomb attacks on hotels frequented by the enemy, 33 hand grenade attacks on a further 33 hotels, 15 arson attacks on German recruiting offices, the gutting by fire of 78 warehouses containing war materials, the destruction of 123 military buses and grenade attacks on '19 busloads of Hitlerites'. In addition, the two groups carried out assassinations of German officers and collaborators, as well as successful grenade attacks on groups of German soldiers and their barracks, numerous train derailments and the destruction of two anti-aircraft guns and 123 military buses. In one derailment alone 14 wagonloads of weapons were destroyed and the line was put out of action for several days.

In total an estimated 3,000 German troops were killed in these attacks, which inflicted a small but significant dent in German morale and demonstrated to occupation forces and the French civilians that an active resistance movement was operating in the capital in defiance of the hated enemy.

Tragically, Lissner and his Parisian comrades were finally betrayed by one of their own superiors, who broke down during interrogation and led the Gestapo to their meeting places. Consequently, many were arrested and those who eluded the Gestapo that October were forced to flee the city. Lissner was among the fortunate few who managed to escape, but while on the run in Douai in the Nord region he saw posters announcing the arrest of 'The Army of Criminals', the name given to the immigrants from Algiers and elsewhere who had formed the Partisans of Paris. Their faces were bruised and swollen from the beatings they had endured.

The Algerian Jewish underground

When Algerian Max Danan was a child he and his friends used the word 'Jew' as a generic curse for anyone they despised. But when Max spat it out during an argument with his father, he was told that he himself was a Jew. Moreover, his uncle, José Aboulker, had been the leader of the Algerian resistance, a movement composed almost entirely of Jews.

'The underground numbered 800 fighters, half of them Jewish,' remembers Jacques Zermati, a former commander of the Algerian Jewish underground. 'But at the moment of truth, 400 of them had cold feet, and just 400 were left – almost all of them Jewish.'

Algerian Jews played a leading role in Operation Torch, the Anglo-American landing in French North Africa which was crucial to the success of a planned pincer movement against the Axis in North Africa. It is an episode which has been largely ignored by historians.

Part of the reason for the 'oversight' was the anti-Semitism of the Vichy regime, which had imposed the anti-Jewish Nuremberg Laws on all Jewish citizens in its colonies. This compelled them to wear the Star of David on their clothes and prevented them from attending universities and entering the professions. As a result, its leaders were averse to giving any credit for the liberation of its colony to Jews, particularly Algerian Jews. This was particularly galling to Zermati and his comrades, who were proud of their French citizenship.

Fortunately, many of the French army officers who were based in North Africa were anti-Vichy and were only too willing to co-operate with the underground, who also had the support of the Free French government in exile led by Charles de Gaulle.

Africa's north-west coast was defended by 50,000 Vichy French and their Axis allies, a sizeable force who would have easily repelled the landings and inflicted severe losses on the invaders. So there was no hope of the resistance overwhelming them or even providing a diversion. Zermati and his comrades were also poorly equipped for such a mission and were lacking in basic weapons training.

'To be honest, we didn't have a clue how to fire a gun,' Zermati later recalled. 'We had a sub-machine gun with six bullets, and they promised to explain to us how to use it, but there was no time – so they never did.'

Their only hope was subterfuge and that particular brand of brazen self-confidence that Jews call chutzpah. They forged orders from a high-ranking Vichy officer giving Algerian resistance leader José Aboulker authority to replace key army personnel with his own men. By this means the resistance were able to take over vital strategic posts, including the communications and command centres, enabling them to countermand any orders given to fire on the approaching armada. This ensured that the Americans could make an unopposed landing on the beaches on 8 November 1942.

Among the top brass who surrendered without a shot being fired was Marshal Pétain's deputy General Alphonse Juin, whose reaction to being duped by 400 Jewish partisans is not recorded.

Chapter Four

REVOLT IN THE EAST

Bulgaria

When Bulgaria's despotic leader Tsar Boris III joined the Axis on 1 March 1941 he did so in the hope that his country would profit from aligning itself with Nazi Germany. With only a token army of 25 poorly armed divisions (a force no larger than that of Belgium) and an obsolete navy and air force, neutral Bulgaria was in no shape to defend itself against the combined might of the Wehrmacht and the Luftwaffe. An alliance seemed to be the only course and in return the Tsar could make a case for the restoration of territory lost to Greece and Turkey in 1919.

The previous September Hitler and his Soviet allies had forced Romania to relinquish its claim to Southern Dobruja, allowing the Bulgarians to march in without firing a shot, so there was

At the height of his power in 1941, Adolf Hitler welcomed Boris III of Bulgaria (centre) to Berchtesgaden.

every chance Boris could pull off a similar coup if he made himself agreeable to Hitler.

All that was asked of the Tsar was that he should allow German 'observers' into his country to make preparations for the invasion of Greece the following spring. The Bulgarian people need have no fear of their German allies, he was told, with the exception of the Jews who would be rounded up and transported to the 'East German territories'.

But this, as it turned out, was something the Bulgarian people were not prepared to accept. Unlike the other Slavic states, there was no history of endemic anti-Semitism in Bulgaria. The population had endured a life of privation and repression and they saw the Jews as fellow citizens who had shared in that deprivation. The Bulgarian army, however, were not so tolerant of the Greeks of Thrace, on whom they attempted to impose their own culture and whom they massacred by the thousand when the population rose up in revolt, leaving the survivors to seek safety in the German-occupied region.

But in Bulgaria the general population protected their own – regardless of their race or religion.

The popular protests against the deportation of the Jews began as soon as the first draft of the anti-Jewish laws was announced. Mass street protests were held to demonstrate public anger at the proposed 'Law in Defence of the Nation', which would divest Bulgarian Jews of their citizenship and basic human rights. The Bulgarian Orthodox Church was among the first voices raised in protest against the draft bill in the belief that it was the 'duty' of the Church to oppose a law that was 'unjust' and not 'in the interests of the nation'. The statement was followed by similar declarations from the representatives of various professional bodies including doctors, lawyers and scientists, all of whom expressed the belief that it would be divisive and prove an indelible stain on the country and its constitution. A spokesman for the Academy of Sciences opposed the law on the grounds that talk of a 'pure race' was a 'mystification' and that such a law would be contrary to the 'culture and dignity of the Bulgarian people'.

Parliament was besieged with letters from thousands of private individuals as resentment swept through society, enraging intellectuals and workers alike. When senior army officers declared their opposition the Tsar and his pro-fascist ministers feared a coup, but they believed the Nazis would come to their aid and implement the law by force, and so they ignored the protests and voted in favour of the bill in December 1940.

Deprived of employment, evicted from their homes and forced to wear a yellow Star of David in public, the plight of the Jews soon aroused the sympathy of Bulgaria's opposition parties. The communist, social-democrat and agrarian parties began a campaign to inform the population of how their Jewish neighbours were suffering under the Tsar. They revealed that plans were being made to transport them to slave labour and extermination camps, which was the fate of the Jews of Poland and the other occupied countries.

Unexpected assistance

Through the underground radio network, clandestine meetings and the underground press established by the anti-fascist Fatherland Front, Bulgarians were informed of the threat posed to their country by their government's alliance with the Nazis. They were told that the Jews would be first to be liquidated, then the intellectuals and the professionals and after that the army would be purged of its officers. Finally, the workers would be enslaved by their new Aryan masters and their Bulgarian collaborators.

By the time the first deportation of 20,000 Jews was announced on 22 February 1943, the majority of Bulgarians were incensed and ready to oppose the order with every means at their disposal. When the day finally came for the round-up, on 24 May, Bulgarian revolutionaries issued a rallying call that brought thousands on to the streets of the capital, Sofia.

> *'Take your stand before your neighbouring Jewish homes and do not let them be led away by force! Hide the children and do not give them to the executioners! Crowd the Jewish quarters and manifest your solidarity with the oppressed Jews!'*

A sizeable crowd then marched on the royal palace, where they were met with violence by the police. Many were arrested but the size of the opposition was sufficient to unnerve the Tsar, who feared a revolution and was forced to rescind the order to round up the Jews.

The empty cattle wagons remained in their sidings.

That summer the Bulgarian resistance gathered momentum, assisted by popular hostility towards the government. Acts of sabotage became more frequent and the partisan movement grew substantially until it was able to offer effective armed opposition to both the Bulgarian army and the German occupation forces, who were unable to join the fight on the Eastern Front because of the activities of the guerrillas.

There were no exclusively Jewish partisan units in Bulgaria but 260 Jews joined the guerrillas, who now numbered 20,000. Of these 125 were killed. However, their contribution to the liberation of the country was later commemorated by the naming of streets in their honour. Of all the occupied countries, Bulgaria is the only one in which almost every city can boast a street named in recognition of the Jewish partisans.

The Bielski brothers

The activities of the three Bielski brothers, the Polish partisans who offered sanctuary to more than 1,200 Polish Jews, including several hundred fighters, in the Naliboki forest in north-west Byelorussia (now known as Belarus), are widely known thanks to the film *Defiance* (2008), starring Daniel Craig, and the book on which it is based. But some Poles claim that the three brothers were not the heroes portrayed in the film and that they were involved in a massacre of Polish anti-Nazi resistance fighters in Naliboki forest on 8 May 1943.

Jack Kagan knows otherwise, for as a 14-year-old boy he lived and fought with them after escaping from a Nazi prison camp with a 21-year-old friend.

> *'Tuvia, Zus and Asael were heroes. They saved my life and so many others. Without them we would all have been killed. They were much more concerned with saving Jews than with killing Nazis. They did not kill innocent people. They killed collaborators who had betrayed the Jews to the Nazis, and any Nazis who threatened their community. The killings were a deterrent aimed at those who thought of selling Jewish lives to the Germans for a sack of potatoes. It was war and they were protecting their people who had*

seen thousands of Jews, including their own families, murdered by the Nazis.'

As for the accusation that they participated in the massacre of Poles, Kagan counters that the Bielskis were 60 km (37 miles) away at that time and that the killings were in fact carried out by pro-Soviet partisans.

Forest sanctuary

Kagan and his friend Pesch had wandered through the forest for five days following their escape, which gives some impression of how vast Naliboki was and how it was possible for the Bielski camp to remain undiscovered for so long, although the settlement was large enough to sustain a bakery, a makeshift hospital and workshops for carpenters, tailors and shoemakers. However, the camp's inhabitants mainly relied on stealing food and clothing or buying these items from local farmers. Though deprived of the most basic facilities they were determined to maintain their dignity and pride. To that end they built a bathhouse, which was used by every inhabitant of the settlement at least once a fortnight – an unheard-of luxury for fighters in the forest.

No moment of that flight from certain death had dimmed with the passing years, for every step had been excruciating. Kagan had recently had all of his toes amputated by the prison camp dentist using pliers, following an earlier escape attempt which had left him with severe frostbite.

REVOLT IN THE EAST

His first sight of his rescuers was when two of the brothers rode up on horseback, sporting machine guns.

> 'I had come from a camp where thousands of Jewish people were being killed by the Germans. And now there were all these fighters, with guns. I felt very proud.
>
> 'There was a great camaraderie at the camp. We were unhappy because so many members of our families, including my mother and sister, had been massacred. But we were happy because we were free and we were fighting back.'

Nazis occupy Byelorussia

Kagan's story is remarkable but probably no more so than those of his compatriots who had been given shelter in the forests of Eastern Europe.

When the Russians occupied Byelorussia in 1939 they behaved as brutally as the Nazis who would follow them two years later. Jack was then ten, the middle-class son of a saddlemaker in Novogrudek whose business was shut down by the Soviet authorities as private enterprise was considered to be against the communist ideology. Although affluent Jews were stripped of their wealth and shipped off to Siberia, the Kagan family were spared their fate, but the respite only lasted until 22 June 1941 when the town was bombed by the Luftwaffe. A fortnight later, the Germans occupied the region and massacred thousands of the region's Jews. Fifty-two were shot in Novogrudek's market square while the German troops looked on. Local musicians were ordered to play Strauss waltzes.

That winter 5,000 more of the region's Jews were forced to march to the killing pits outside the town, where they were shot. Kagan's family were spared because they were skilled leather workers, and so were useful to their new masters, but by May 1943 even they were deemed expendable. Kagan was interned in a forced labour camp, his mother and his sister, his only sibling, were shot and his father was transported to a concentration camp. Now alone in the world, his only thoughts were of escape and revenge.

Tunnel escape route

That autumn he put every last ounce of his failing energy into helping his fellow prisoners dig a 250-metre tunnel under the camp from their barracks to the perimeter wire, which they reinforced with wood and illuminated with electric lighting. Mercifully, it remained undetected until the night of 26 September, when all 232 slave workers were ready to escape. But in cutting the power to the watchtower searchlights, they had unwittingly left themselves without sufficient light. Seventy of their number became disorientated in the dark and blundered into the sentries, who shot them.

Kagan and his friend Pesch evaded the pursuing SS for five long and nerve-jangling days, surviving on scraps provided by compassionate peasants. After covering 40 km (25 miles), with Kagan in considerable pain from the wounds to his feet, they finally came upon the house of a man they had been told could take them to the Bielski brothers. But the house was gone, burned down by the Nazis and there was no trace of its owner. Later they learned that he and his wife had both been burned alive inside the building.

A group of partisans from various fighting units, including the Bielski group and escapees from the Mir ghetto, on guard duty in the Naliboki forest (now Belarus), 1944.

Fortunately, they came across a former neighbour whom they could trust and he offered to take them to Naliboki forest, where they could make contact with the partisans.

Out for revenge

But there were many groups who sought sanctuary in the forests of Eastern Europe, among them the group formed by Dr Atlas, who was driven by the desire to avenge his murdered family. Another group, led by 'Uncle' Misha Gildenman, included a 12-year-old boy who capitalized on his Aryan appearance to lure a group of Nazi officers into a lethal trap.

In Croatia 1,600 Jews joined the partisans, but not all as fighters. Some chose to serve as doctors and nurses or even cooks, anything to contribute to the war against the oppressor.

Romanian Jews were unable to form resistance groups because the totalitarian regime of President Ion Antonescu had crushed all opposition before his country allied itself with the Nazis. Despite this, the surviving Jews managed to sabotage Antonescu's Aryanization of Jewish urban property and businesses. In Byelorussia, an estimated 15,000 Jews joined the partisans, while the capital, Minsk, witnessed the largest numerical resistance to Nazi occupation.

Ironically, Ukrainian Jews welcomed the Nazis as liberators after suffering generations of persecution sanctioned by the Catholic church. Consequently, they fought only for survival rather than to free their country.

Hannah Senesh

Among the most courageous Jews were those who chose to leave the comparative safety of what was then Palestine to join the fight against fascism in Europe.

Hungarian partisan and poet Hannah Senesh had emigrated to the future Jewish homeland in 1939 to escape Nazi persecution, but then chose to enlist in the British army in 1943 as a paratrooper. The following year she was dropped into occupied Yugoslavia and joined Tito's partisans in the task of organizing resistance activities and rescuing Allied soldiers and airmen trapped behind enemy

Hannah Senesh abandoned the relative safety of Palestine to fight the Nazis in Yugoslavia.

lines. But while attempting to cross the border into Hungary so that she could assist in the rescue of Hungarian Jews she was captured, imprisoned and tortured. She was executed on 7 November 1944 without betraying her comrades.

Poland

The Jews of Poland were no strangers to persecution. Neither were their brothers and sisters in the other countries that Hitler's henchmen would overrun. But of all the communities in Europe that fell under the Nazi scourge, the fate of Poland's three million Jews is particularly poignant, for it was for Poland that the Allies went to war. And it was Poland which emerged from that conflict under the shadow of an equally oppressive regime, which treated the survivors of Treblinka and Auschwitz as cruelly as the Germans had done.

The Jews of Poland had endured hardship, poverty and discrimination for generations. They lived in a state of perpetual insecurity, surrounded by antagonistic neighbours who regarded all Jews with suspicion and the wealthier ones with envy. Anti-Semitism was endemic and openly condoned by the authorities, who were unashamedly and demonstrably anti-Semitic.

Polish partisan Harold Werner recalled being chased through the streets of Warsaw by a gang of anti-Semites in the years before the war, accompanied by his 16-year-old brother Moishe, and seeing a Polish policeman turn his back to give the thugs a free hand to beat them both up.

When the Germans invaded in September 1939 it was as if their persecutors had found new allies. Werner's fledgling business was destroyed in the bombing and then he was forced to leave a bread line on more than one occasion when his fellow Poles told the Germans that he was not entitled to any.

Murdered by their neighbours

It was incidents such as this that forced the young and able-bodied Jews of Poland to flee into the forests and form partisan groups, painful though it was for them to leave their families behind. In addition to the physical privations and the ever-present threat of discovery, they endured mental anguish, tormented by the unknown fate of their families and the numerous life or death decisions that beset them. Should they attempt to cross into Russia or remain in occupied Poland? If they remained, where was it best to hide out – the city, the villages or the forests? Where could they find shelter and who could they trust to supply them with the basic needs of survival? All this before they even contemplated how they could obtain weapons and ammunition, how they could strike back and what the cost of those attacks might be in terms of German reprisals.

Werner (whose real name was Herschel Zimmerman) chose to leave Warsaw and seek shelter in Hola, a village to the east of the capital near the River Bug which bordered Russia. But nowhere was truly safe. The local farmers refused to give him food and one told him that in a neighbouring village the inhabitants had killed both the farmer and the Jew that he had sheltered.

Werner was fortunate. He found lodgings and work in Hola with a family who owned a small mill used for grinding poppy seed and linseed oil. But within weeks the Germans began scouring the region for Russian soldiers who had evaded capture after the rout of the Soviet army. That first winter Werner witnessed how they treated their former allies.

One day, while travelling to Włodawa to deliver grain, he came upon thousands of Russian prisoners shivering and starving in an open field surrounded by barbed wire. The Germans evidently had no intention of treating them humanely, according to the Geneva Convention. It served them better if the prisoners died from hypothermia and malnutrition.

The Jews would be next. But before they could be rounded up and transported to the ghetto at Włodawa, Werner and a small group of Jewish inhabitants from Hola escaped into the forest where they hoped to live off the land and from where they could launch their raids against the invaders.

But their former neighbours had other ideas. Shortly after they left the village, Werner and two of his friends went foraging for food.

While they were away a mob of 50 villagers organized a manhunt and armed themselves with pitchforks, clubs and other crude weapons. They soon found the Jews' hiding place in the woods and forced them to walk to Sosnowica, where they turned them over to the Germans who executed them on the spot.

It was not the only incident of that nature that Werner heard about. In nearby Zamołodycze, Ukrainian villagers rounded up their Jewish neighbours then sent for the Germans, who executed them in front of those who had betrayed them. The son of the village shoemaker attempted to escape, but the villagers caught him and handed him over to the Germans, who promptly shot him.

Strain of survival

With every new outrage Werner's group grew in number, reinforced by the survivors and those Jews from the surrounding countryside who could see that their only chance lay in joining the insurgents in the forests. At the mercy of the elements and deprived of the most basic facilities they were reduced to scavenging for scraps of discarded food on the outskirts of the neighbouring villages and farms, foraging for berries and hunting like wolves for rabbits and other small animals. And still they kept their humanity. But not all groups fighting the Germans could be trusted to conduct themselves like civilized people.

While Werner's group were still without arms or ammunition, a group of 40 Russian partisans descended on them and raped the women. There was nothing Werner and the other men could do.

Other Russians they encountered proved to be true allies in their fight against the common enemy, but there was always the threat that they would be discovered or that the weather would wear down their resolve. On one occasion a party of German hunters stumbled upon their camp by chance and began shooting indiscriminately. Fortunately, a blizzard forced them to abandon the chase, but when the weather cleared Werner and his men discovered that a dozen of their comrades had frozen to death.

The constant strain proved too much for some, who conceded defeat and walked out of the woods and towards the ghetto, even though they faced certain death on the road or, if not, at journey's end.

Once they had arms their priority was to sabotage German

troop and ammunition trains, but they would not forget nor forgive the villagers who had betrayed them and their comrades. When they were sure of the identity of the informers and those who had led the manhunts for Jews they carried out reprisals, which had the effect of deterring future manhunts.

Swampland stronghold

Any reservations they might have had regarding the assassination of civilians was dispelled when they recalled that these were the men who had turned their Jewish neighbours over to the enemy. Several of the Ukrainians attempted to deny their crimes, but were betrayed by the fact that they were wearing the boots they had taken from the bodies of murdered Jews.

By the late spring of 1943 Werner could count about 120 men and women among his fellow fighters, but only about 25 were armed, and so were limited to hit and run assaults on a local German garrison, which was manned by fewer than a dozen soldiers. In order to inflict significant damage on enemy troop trains, bridges and other strategically important targets they would have to join a larger group. They contacted a unit which operated in Parczew forest and guarded hundreds of Jewish families who had fled into the impenetrable woodland and lived on natural islands surrounded by swamp. These camps, or Tabor, as they were known, were organized like small villages and had their own cook, who would be responsible for the distribution of their most precious commodity – food.

The Tabor was sanctuary only as long as the swamp remained

inaccessible, but the long, hot, dry summer of 1943 left the inhabitants vulnerable to German patrols. While the partisans were away on a raid, the Germans attacked, massacring 75 old men, women and children. Some of the boys and old men had weapons and managed to kill their attackers before they themselves were killed. As Werner noted: 'This was their first opportunity to avenge the cruelties that had been committed against their families. Unfortunately, for many of them, this opportunity was also their last.'

One incident in particular serves to highlight the barbarity and duplicity of the Germans and their Ukrainian and Latvian paramilitary collaborators.

Among the slave workers in a Nazi labour camp at Adampol were more than a hundred Jewish women, who had been spared the gas chambers at Sobibór in order to serve their Ukrainian and Latvian guards and the German soldiers. None of their abusers had any misgivings about using the Jewish females for their sexual gratification, despite rabid Nazi anti-Semitic propaganda and the infamous Nuremberg Laws forbidding Aryans from having sexual relations with Jews.

Raids on the Germans

In three audacious raids Werner and comrades were able to breach the barbed wire fence and smuggle out more than a hundred women and young girls before the Germans closed the camp and murdered the remaining prisoners.

But their limits were soon brought home to them in a heartrending incident which saw the group powerless to rescue the inmates of Sobibór. They had seriously considered a raid on the death camp in the hope of liberating some of the prisoners, but a closer inspection of the heavily guarded compound convinced them that it would be a futile gesture and certain suicide for those who attempted to breach the perimeter. All they could do was fire a few rounds into the air before retreating, in the hope that it would give hope to those inside and let them know that someone was aware of their plight.

While the accounts of the unit's raids on German military installations testify to their courage in the face of insurmountable odds, it is the descriptions of individual suffering which prove the most moving.

During a raid on the German grain stores they saw a figure crawling on all fours from the burning barn. At first they were not even sure he was a human being. Cadaverously thin, he had lost all his teeth and lacked the strength to stand up. He was covered in hair down to his waist and his clothes were in shreds. But they dragged him to safety. Once clear of the farm and their pursuers, they cut his hair and cleaned him up as best they could. Werner was shocked when he recognized this feral creature as his former friend, the nephew of the farmer whose barn they had set alight. He was delirious from hunger and though they tried to feed him he couldn't hold down solid food and died a few days later.

It was this incident that had brought tears to the eyes of Holocaust historian Martin Gilbert when he read the account of Werner's wartime experiences at Yad Vashem, the Holocaust memorial library in Jerusalem. But tears would not do the dead any good. Only preserving the account of what they had been forced to endure would serve as testimony to the cruelty that men can do to one another.

Werner appears to have been a man not given to holding grudges when the war was won, but he gives the impression that he reserved a particular aversion for those of his fellow Poles who took advantage of the war to hound and murder their Jewish countrymen. In the spring of 1944, when the Germans were in retreat on the Eastern Front, Werner's unit was part of a force of 400 partisans under the command of Chiel Grynszpan, which carried out hit and run raids on numerous road and rail bridges and lethal reprisals on Polish collaborators. But even then, with the Germans on the defensive and few enemy patrols venturing into the forests, the Jews were still being murdered – this time by the official Polish partisans, known as the Armia Krajowa, under the leadership of the Polish government in exile in London.

Thirteen Soviet-backed partisans, including five Jews from Werner's group, were murdered after being surrounded by the Krajowa forces. Some months later Werner's unit came to the aid of the Krajowa, who were surrounded by Germans, but even this did not deter them from subsequently killing unarmed Jews and rival Jewish partisans whenever they came upon them.

Thankless sacrifice

For two gruelling years, the Jewish partisans of Poland had endured so much and made a small but significant contribution to the

German defeat, but even so there would be no heroes' welcome for them. One of Werner's friends, Abram Bochian, who had witnessed the death of his entire family in the forest campaign, returned home after the war only to be murdered by his neighbours. But the cruellest blow of all was reserved for Werner's own homecoming. On his return he was informed by a neighbour that both of his younger brothers, 13-year-old Motel and 17-year-old Moishe, had left the ghetto and taken refuge in the woods only to be betrayed by a former neighbour. He had told them to wait in his barn while he brought them food and had then returned with a gang of thugs who beat both boys to death with their clubs.

Werner's story – sadly typical of thousands of Jewish resistance fighters – might have remained untold were it not for the chance discovery of a written account that he had been asked to contribute to the archive of Yad Vashem during a gathering of survivors in June 1981.

It was there, the following year, that Holocaust historian Martin Gilbert was told of its existence by the archivist, who had recognized its significance. It was the only first-hand account of Jewish resistance in the Włodawa region of Poland. Gilbert then insisted that the 64-year-old Werner set down the full story of his wartime experiences for his family, who had little idea of their father and grandfather's story, as much as for the outside world. Although he was by now frail and in poor health, Werner completed his memoir *Fighting Back* just two weeks before his death in November 1989.

Little Wanda

She couldn't have been more than 16 and with her slim figure, penetrating blue eyes and plaited blonde hair she was very pretty and every young soldier's fantasy. The guards at Gestapo Headquarters in Warsaw exchanged looks that said: 'Whoever she is here to see, he is a lucky man.'

She asked them for the room number of a senior officer whom she wished to see 'on a private matter' and they let her pass. What they would have given to exchange places with him right now?

But when she reached his door, she didn't wait to be invited in. He rose from behind his desk ready to bark at her for intruding. No one entered his office without being admitted. But she was pretty. It was the last thought he had, for the next moment she had drawn a revolver from her handbag and fired. He slumped back lifeless in his chair.

If she was lucky, no one would have heard the shot. The walls were thick and the clamour of typewriters in the adjoining offices might have been loud enough to drown the sound. But she was out in the corridor and striding towards the exit before anyone could react. She had been trained well and it was not her first killing.

The guards at the main gate were too surprised by her sudden reappearance to challenge her. By the time they had been alerted, she was long gone.

The Gestapo called her 'Little Wanda with the braids' and they offered a substantial reward for her capture – 150,000 zlotys ($40,000). Her real name was Niuta Teitelboim and she had been an active member of the left-wing student group at Warsaw University before the German invasion in September 1939. As a member of the ghetto underground, she smuggled in arms for the beleaguered inhabitants and became their most valuable contact with the People's Guard, as the official Polish underground was known.

But she was not content with the role of *kasharivot*, as the messengers and smugglers who provided a vital lifeline to the outside world were known, dangerous as it was. She wanted to bring the war to the Germans, the occupation forces whose presence had deprived her of a future in her own country and robbed her fellow Jews of their rightful place in Polish society. Within a very short time she became a weapons expert, but it was her courage that her comrades most admired. That and her miraculous ability to repeatedly circumvent the cordon with which the Germans had surrounded the ghetto in July 1942, in preparation for the liquidation of its inhabitants.

Not only had she led other Jews to safety, but that autumn she had managed to take part in the sabotage of the main railway lines, preventing German troops, tanks and ammunition from being transported to the Eastern Front. After the Germans hanged 50 Poles as a warning to the population, the People's Guard avenged their public execution with simultaneous attacks on a café and coffee house frequented by Wehrmacht and Gestapo officers. They killed 30 in total before bombing the offices of the *New Warsaw Courier*, the official Nazi-controlled newspaper.

The Germans had also imposed a fine of one million zlotys ($276,000) on the Poles because of the sabotage of the railway, which Wanda and her comrades recovered in an audacious daylight raid on the Communal Bank on 30 November.

When the Germans began the liquidation of the ghetto on 19 April 1943 Wanda was among the group who attacked a German artillery battery and put it out of action. Sadly, in July the Gestapo discovered her hiding place and before she could take the poison she always carried with her, she was captured. Though tortured she refused to divulge the names of her accomplices and shortly before her death she managed to smuggle out a message to the resistance assuring them that nothing could make her betray them.

After the war she was posthumously awarded the Grunwald Cross, Poland's highest combat honour.

Witness in Warsaw

Ben Kamm was 19 when he and his extended family were herded into the ghetto which the Germans had euphemistically called 'The Jewish Residential Quarter'. He and his four younger brothers were no strangers to anti-Semitism, having been taunted almost daily by their neighbours who resented the family's comparative prosperity. The boys' father managed a profitable meat packaging business and their grandfather owned the spacious property that the whole family inhabited in some comfort.

'We were abused every single day,' Ben quickly remembered, 'they called me "dirty Jew, lousy Jew" and every single day we had to fight.'

But now they were physically isolated from their fellow citizens and officially outcasts in their own country, without rights or entitlements of any kind.

There would be no sympathy shown to the Kamms and their kind by the Polish population and there was no hope of assistance from these same people later, when the remnants of the Jewish community were reduced to starvation within sight and sound of their former neighbours.

The Jews of Warsaw were reduced to an allowance of 187 calories per person per day, a fraction of what would be needed to sustain life. It was certainly not enough to stave off the gnawing hunger pangs which forced many to risk summary execution for smuggling the barest essentials into the ghetto. Without adequate food, the ghetto population was prey to malnutrition and disease. It was common to see corpses lying in the open, in doorways and in the gutters, where they were ignored and left for days by people who would previously have been distressed to see a dead dog.

Passing for Aryan

Ben Kamm could not sit idly by while his proud parents and his beloved grandparents and brothers deteriorated with each passing day. It was not in his nature to see people suffer and do nothing about it. He was young and believed himself invincible. They might catch others, but not him. He was too quick and clever to be caught. Besides, with his blond hair, blue eyes and immaculate Polish accent he could pass as an Aryan, just as his aunt was doing in the Polish neighbourhood that she had refused to leave that winter.

She had renounced her Jewish upbringing by marrying a Polish army officer, but Ben was certain that if he could contact her and appeal to her for help she would not abandon her sister's family in their time of need. In fact, she did more than he could have hoped for.

Not only did she regularly supply her nephew with fresh meat, but she enlisted the aid of her son who owned a printing works and offered to print forged identity papers, which Ben gladly distributed.

The following spring of 1941 brought rumours of guerrillas staging hit and run raids against the Germans near Lublin. Normally it would have entailed a three-hour journey by road or rail. But Ben would have to travel on foot unless he wanted to risk having his forged papers scrutinized. Besides, he had convinced nine of his friends to join him and they could not run the risk of arrest.

'We thought the war would be over in a couple of months.

Russia and England and France are in the war, they're going to crush Hitler. So we didn't expect this, the war to last.'

An embittered young man

They left the ghetto without anything to contribute to the partisans' campaign other than youthful enthusiasm. Fortunately, their first attempt to contact the partisans brought them into contact with Grzegorz Korczyński, a partisan commander and former Polish officer who was in need of recruits even more than he was in need of weapons. Arms were easily procured from the Polish police, who could be ambushed as they rode their bicycles through the woods.

Once they had a weapon they could use it to obtain more by holding up farmers, who always had a rifle or shotgun with them. As a bonus they might persuade them to donate some food and drink to the cause or even a night's shelter in their barn with their captive host for company. But the novelty of living rough soon evaporated.

They made the fatal mistake of trusting one of the local farmers, who took the opportunity to betray them to the Polish police. Five of Ben's friends were shot dead before they could escape from the barn and the remaining three returned to the ghetto rather than risk being killed. Ben was left alone with Korczyński's unit, determined to see the fight out to the bitter end. But there were other privations to be endured that he could not have foreseen.

'During the day we talked about how to ambush the Germans,

how to get food and how to get rid of the lice. One million lice! Everybody had lice. Do you know that for three years I never took a shower or bath? I didn't know what a bath was.'

But he was soon persuaded to make the hazardous journey back to Warsaw after receiving a distressing message from his mother informing him of the desperate situation in the ghetto. The scenes he witnessed on his return shocked him to the core. His family were living in a single room they shared with three other families. And children were begging in the street among the dead and the dying. After two days, he reluctantly decided to leave, believing that his brothers would be safer in the city than living hand to mouth in the forest.

'I think that the human mind cannot comprehend what happened. That they were going to take people and gas them and kill them by the millions; it didn't even come into my mind.'

On his return to the partisans he was no longer an idealistic youth but an embittered young man intent on avenging the cruelty that had been inflicted on his family and friends. He appeared to have lost all sense of personal danger and threw himself into every operation with reckless courage.

Disillusionment

A particularly hazardous mission involved the destruction of the Janów Lubelski labour camp and the freeing of its 1,000 Jewish slave workers. The partisans had to lie still and silent for most of the day until darkness offered the cover they needed to approach the perimeter and kill the guards. Although the operation was successful, the awful nature of the prisoners' predicament was made plain.

'We couldn't take them with us,' Ben later wrote. 'We didn't have the guns. We didn't have the food. They were scared. They didn't know what to do, where to go. They stayed there. Next day Germans came in, took them someplace else.'

Only a hundred or so had the courage and the strength to run into the forest and fend for themselves. And only 60 of these avoided being recaptured or shot. As inconceivable as it might seem to us, the prisoners reasoned that the Germans needed them to finish the work they had started and would provide them with food and shelter, which is all they could think of at the time.

It was the beginning of Ben's disillusionment with that particular partisan unit. The crisis came after its commander ordered 16 Polish soldiers, all of them Jews, to be shot for refusing to hand over the money they were carrying. Korczyński justified their execution by claiming that his group needed the money to buy provisions and weapons and that their refusal meant they were not willing to obey orders. Ben was not convinced.

'Because he killed Jews, I was angry. Eventually, he would have done it to me.'

Joins the Russians

Ben persuaded a number of the group to leave and shortly afterwards they found themselves fighting their former comrades, including Korczyński. The gun battle saw several dead and wounded on both sides. It was clear that the rival units could not operate in the same region without further bloodshed, so Ben and his group walked for two weeks to join a Russian group in the Polish Ukraine that they had heard were looking for experienced fighters.

'It was winter and bitter, bitter cold. I wore a coat made out of sheepskin. A long coat. And rags around my feet, so my feet shouldn't freeze. The worst thing was rain. After rain you're soaking wet. I mean wet. And you never take a shower, you never bathe. You stink! Like a dead animal. Just like a dead animal.'

The Russian group was in fact a small army of 1,600 men who were regularly supplied by the Soviet air force and lacked for nothing other than a barracks and a warm bed.

'We had four different radios. If we needed help from Russia, the airplanes came. We used to get drops with ammunitions, with guns, every day. They had five doctors. They had a place where they used to fix shoes, fix clothing. We had the orchestra. We used to dance.'

Their living quarters, however, were rough and ready. 'We dug a hole with about 50 people and covered it up with trees. Like a room. You lay down and slept on your straw.'

Their commander was General Fyodorov, who allowed Ben and his men to remain a separate unit within his brigade. The general knew from experience that men who had fought along-side each other had formed a bond that made them a more effective unit than those who merely shared a uniform and a common enemy.

One tyranny for another

'They taught us like a regular army ... to use a machine gun, to use grenades, to place mines. ... Our main job was to destroy the rail lines going to the Eastern Front.'

In this they were uncommonly successful, claiming 549 trains by the winter of 1943.

There was little the Germans could do to protect the trains as they were now in retreat and had no men to spare to go on the offensive against the Russian partisans, who were fighting on familiar territory and were well-equipped and substantial in number. The Germans could never be sure where the train would be attacked as the partisans could be hiding anywhere along the route ready to throw a magnetic mine against the engine, which exploded before the locomotive could stop. Once the engine was wrecked, the troops were easy prey and the shipment of arms and other material could be carried back to the camp.

That December there was an unexpected windfall when one of the derailed trains spilled its freight of Christmas presents on to the snow. Gifts of cake and warm winter clothing sent by the soldiers' families were eagerly taken by those who had not seen their families all year and would probably never see them again. For the non-Jewish fighters of the Fyodorov Brigade, it was a bitter sweet reminder of what they were fighting for.

In 1944 the order came for all Polish partisans to return to their mother country in order to arm and organize their compatriots to repel the fascist invaders. After walking hundreds of kilometres from Ukraine, the 1,200 former fighters of the Fyodorov Brigade – many of them Jews – found themselves fighting side by side with those who had refused to aid them when they and their families were starving in the ghettos. But they had to put their enmity to one side to win the final battle ahead of the Soviet advance.

Ben was in the newly formed Wanda Wasilewska Brigade, which found itself surrounded by thousands of German soldiers in the last weeks of the war. But the Poles were prepared, having had prior warning of the attack from Russian radio. The battle lasted 16 hours with both sides taking heavy casualties, but eventually the Germans were beaten back.

Soon afterwards Germany surrendered and the Soviet forces occupied Poland. The country for whom the Western world had gone to war had exchanged one tyranny for another.

But Ben was in no doubt at all that his war was a just and necessary fight against evil.

'I can't forgive people [who] killed innocent babies, innocent women, innocent people.... They killed the best of us. I am just very sorry that more of our Jewish boys and girls did not have the opportunity to do the same as I did.'

Chapter Five

THE WARSAW UPRISING

'The most difficult struggle of all is the one within
ourselves. Let us not get accustomed and adjusted to these
conditions. The one who adjusts ceases to discriminate between
good and evil. He becomes a slave in body and soul.'
Mordechai Anielewicz, Warsaw ghetto resistance leader

In October 1940, the Jews of Warsaw were ordered to pack their
belongings, but only as much as could be carried in a suitcase,
and move into the slum district of Muranów in the city centre,
where the largest concentration of the capital's Jewish population
had lived before the war.

The ghetto was bisected by the main east–west thoroughfare
of Chlodna Street and ringed with a newly erected three-metre-
high wall topped with barbed wire and broken glass.

All 450,000 of the city's Jews were now crowded into 73 streets covering just over three square kilometres (one square mile) with seven or more people sharing a room.

The cynicism of the Nazi gangster state was without precedent. Having evicted all Jews in the city from their homes, confiscated their possessions and corralled them into a confined space, they proceeded to extort every zloty from them by threats and intimidation. The Jews were made to pay for every malicious act of humiliation, from the building of the ghetto wall to the petrol used to burn down the synagogue on Stawki Street, on the pretext that it was a health hazard. When the Germans took hostages in reprisal for some perceived act of defiance they demanded a ransom of 10,000 zlotys per man. Invariably they had no intention of releasing the hostages. It was simply a ruse to torment their victims. The hostages would be shot anyway.

Jewish council inaction

And still the Jewish council headed by Adam Czerniaków refused to hear the entreaties from resistance leaders such as Yitzhak 'Antek' Zuckerman and Mordechai Anielewicz, who advocated fighting back, even if it would be with fists and bricks. The argument against such action was always the same – that it would provoke the Germans into exacting ever more terrible reprisals. Zuckerman, Anielewicz and others in the Jewish Fighting Organization argued that it made no sense to appease their would-be murderers and that if they were going to die they should at least be given the chance to die with dignity and with honour and not go as 'Sheep to the slaughter', to quote Abba Kovner, leader of the Vilna partisan organization.

Czerniaków could not be swayed by the words of the resistance fighters, but when he failed to persuade the Germans to spare the orphans from transportation to Treblinka he took his own life on 22 July 1942 by taking cyanide. His own wife was among the 100 hostages that the Germans had taken to ensure his compliance. His death was received with resignation by one of the resistance fighters, who condemned Czerniaków for not taking several Germans with him.

Mr Doctor and the orphans

If those in the ghetto who opposed fighting back did so in the belief that they might spare the children, they were mistaken. Among the first to be taken on 6 August were the orphans from the Janusz Korczak orphanage (the exact number is not known, only that between 192 and 196 children were transported that day) who were accompanied by their teacher, Henryk Goldszmit. Pan Doktor, as he was affectionately known to the children, was a paediatrician and a successful children's author who had adopted the pen name of Korczak after a well-known character in a children's book. He had devoted his life to promoting children's rights, giving them their own parliament and newspaper in the institution and advocating a strictly secular education. On the day he steeled himself and his assistants to march the children to the trains, he was repeatedly offered the chance of a safe passage to safety, but he refused.

The children were dressed in their best clothes, carrying knapsacks and clutching favourite toys. They marched out in twos, holding their neighbour by the hand. 'Mr Doctor' had told them that they were going on a special outing and must be on their best behaviour. They would be visiting a beautiful country with flowers and trees and so they should sing on the way to the train. They were never seen again.

The deportations begin

That winter the ghetto's unofficial diarist, Emanuel Ringelblum, wrote:

'Whomever you talk to, you hear the same cry: The resettlement never should have been permitted. We should have run into the street, set fire to everything in sight, have torn down the walls, and escaped to the Other Side. The Germans would have taken their revenge. It would have cost tens of thousands of lives, but not 300,000. Now we are ashamed of ourselves, disgraced in our own eyes, and in the eyes of the world, where our docility has earned us nothing. This must not be repeated now. We must put up a resistance, defend ourselves against the enemy, man and child.'

When the deportations began the Germans had promised bread and marmalade to all those who reported to the assembly area on Umschlagplatz for deportation, knowing that the Jews would see it as proof that they were to be resettled, for who would give food to those they were intending to kill?

The ploy was successful to a degree, until the resistance sent one of their own men to follow the train to Treblinka. He reported back that the railway workers had told him that the trains always returned empty, that no provisions were sent in quantity to feed that number of people, that no facilities were being built for the new arrivals and that the camp was eerily quiet for a supposed work and resettlement centre.

The only evidence of activity was the acrid stench of burning flesh, which could be smelt for miles in every direction. It was the one thing that the Germans could not control. There was no other possible explanation: the Jews were being exterminated. In the first seven weeks of the ghetto being established, 265,000 people had gone to their deaths, leaving just 60,000 to await their turn.

The brutal truth

The Nazis' greatest ally in their systematic annihilation of the Jews was the unwillingness of the victims to believe that such a thing was possible in the civilized world of the 20th century. They could not imagine that anyone would hate them to the extent of planning the systematic murder of every single Jew in Europe, be they man, woman or child. Once the brutal truth had sunk in, those who now awaited their fate behind the ghetto walls knew that they would die, but at least now they could choose how they would meet their end.

Prior to this moment, the various factions within the ghetto (including the Jewish Military Union, which was the first proactive Jewish organization to call for armed resistance after the fall of Poland and the first to form itself into fighting units), had disagreed over how they should respond to German commands. Each group had its own political and ideological philosophy, but now they were forced to set those aside for a common purpose – opposing their extinction. Members of the opposing Zionist associations, the communists and the Jewish Bund were finally in agreement, but it would mean nothing unless they could obtain the weapons to defend themselves.

Obtaining weapons

According to Marek Edelman, a survivor of the Warsaw ghetto uprising:

> 'The Bundists [Jewish Socialists] did not wait for the Messiah, nor did they plan to leave for Palestine. They believed that Poland was their country and they fought for a just, socialist Poland, in which each nationality would have its own cultural autonomy, and in which minorities' rights would be guaranteed.'

Representatives were sent to plead with the Polish Home Army outside the city, but they refused on the grounds that weapons would be wasted on untrained street fighters. They were also fearful of what might happen if the rising was successful. Other Jewish ghettos in Poland might rise up and this would provoke the Germans into widespread retaliation against the resistance throughout Poland. The Jews would have to buy weapons from the Polish population (a precarious transaction at the best of times) and smuggle them into the ghetto. Once they were armed, they could take more from the Germans they had killed. There would be no help from the Allies or anyone else. They were on their own as they had always been.

Jan Karski

The Jewish resistance in occupied Europe was pitifully short of weapons and its members were fighting against time as much as the Germans. Every day that passed saw their number diminished, their ammunition depleted and thousands more of their people exterminated in Hitler's death camps. Their most potent weapon was information, specifically proof of what was happening to the Jews of Europe under Nazi tyranny. Only with Allied intervention could they hope to stop their wholesale destruction.

To that end they enlisted the help of Jan Karski, a member of the Polish underground, who was smuggled into the Warsaw ghetto in 1942 and into what he thought was the Belzec death camp (but which may have been the Izbica transit camp). Disguised as an Estonian guard, he was there to obtain evidence so that he could plead on the

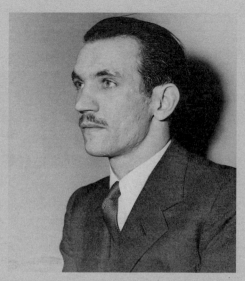

Jan Karski sought to infiltrate the death camps to gain evidence of the Nazis' atrocities to present to the British government.

Jews' behalf with the Polish government in exile in London and the British government.

As the first eyewitness to the Holocaust, he knew his account would be questioned or greeted with suspicion, and so he took with him a roll of microfilm hidden inside the handle of a razor, on which was detailed testimony he had collected from other eyewitnesses.

Karski described the Warsaw ghetto as a living cemetery. 'Everywhere there was hunger, misery, the atrocious stench of decomposing bodies, the pitiful moans of dying children.'

In what had once been a public park he passed mothers cradling their emaciated children.

'Children, every bone in their skeletons showing through their taut skins, played in heaps and swarms. "They play before they die", I heard my companion on the left say, his voice breaking with emotion. Without thinking – the words escaping even before the thought had crystallized – I said: "But these children are not playing – they only make believe it is play".'

He had seen two 'rosy-cheeked' Nazi youths laughing as they fired indiscriminately at the inhabitants. 'The shot rang out ... Then the terrible cry of a man in agony. The boy who had fired ... shouted with joy.'

In what he believed was Belzec, east of Warsaw, he saw a train being loaded 'to bursting' with its human cargo – the floor had been dusted with quicklime to burn the dying and the dead. It took four days for some of them to die, 'the flesh eaten from their bones ... '.

'The Bund leader had warned me that if I lived to a hundred I would never forget some of the things I saw. He did not exaggerate ... The military rule stipulates that a freight wagon may carry eight horses or forty soldiers ... The Germans had simply issued orders to the effect that 120–130 Jews had to

enter each wagon. The people were then left in the train carriages until they died.

'I know that many people will not believe me, will not be able to believe me, will think I exaggerate or invent. But I saw it.'

His report and an account of his experiences, including his treacherous journey through occupied Europe, was published in 1944 as *Story of a Secret State*. It sold 400,000 copies in the first three months. However, his attempt to persuade the exiled Polish prime minister, General Sikorski, the British foreign secretary, Anthony Eden, and President Franklin D. Roosevelt to act failed to induce them to provide aid to the Jewish fighting organizations or to order the bombing of the camps and the railway network.

The Allies expressed their doubts about the scale of the atrocities, but they took Karski's report seriously and discussed it at the highest level. Eden presented it to the War Cabinet who decided that they could not recommend bombing the camps on the grounds that the resulting death of prisoners would be detrimental to the Allied cause. There were also logistical problems concerning the distance the bombers would have to fly and their inability to locate specific targets at high altitude. Flying lower would carry a greater risk for the crews. Had Karski been able to provide proof of the existence of the gas chambers he might have convinced them to act, but he had no knowledge of them at the time. The Allies made their decision not to attack the camps on the understanding that they were slave labour camps and that no mass killings were taking place there on a daily basis. They reassured Karski that they were doing all they could to bring about the end of Nazi Germany and that the liberation of the camps and ghettos was only a matter of time.

But time was something the Jews had little of.

The battle begins

The ghetto fighters were acutely aware of the odds they were up against. Ringelblum wrote: 'We took stock of our position and saw that this was a struggle between a fly and an elephant. But our national dignity dictated to us that the Jews must offer resistance and not allow themselves to be led wantonly to slaughter.'

The first act of the uprising was to deal with the traitors who had betrayed their own people, specifically the Jewish police who could not be trusted to keep silent or stand aside while the underground laid their plans for the defence of the ghetto.

At that time the Jewish Military Association had about 400 fighters and the Jewish Fighting Organization about 600, with at least double that number belonging to small independent groups. Between them they had less than a dozen guns, although they would soon acquire a small arsenal after buying weapons from Polish civilians and some German soldiers who could be bought for a price. They would have to make their own explosives by filling empty bottles with any inflammable liquids they could find.

Meanwhile the entire population of the ghetto was marshalled into preparing the defences for a siege. In the words of Mordekhai Lanski:

'*The entire population, young and old, were busy creating hiding places, particularly underground. To all intents and purposes the ghetto appeared to be a military camp. In the courtyards one could see Jews carrying sacks of sand, bricks and mortar. Work was carried out day and night. The bakeries, in particular, were heavily frequented, as large quantities of bread were needed to prepare rusks [which could be stored for long periods of time without spoiling]. The women worked ceaselessly, kneading dough, preparing loaves of bread and making noodles. As they worked, carrying the dough to the bakeries, their faces bore an expression of exhilarated tension and an almost religious anxiety; they were preparing for what was to come. No one considered going to Treblinka willingly. These people, survivors of previous deportations, now prepared everything needed to survive in hiding for months.*'

Early Jewish victories

On 18 January 1943, the first of a series of isolated and seemingly random attacks on German soldiers took place as a spontaneous reaction to Nazi brutality.

The initial skirmish centred on Mila and Zamenhof streets and lasted for four days, after which the Germans withdrew, leaving the ghetto fighters in a state of euphoria.

Recounting the episode, Ber Mark said: 'In the four days of fighting, we had made up for the shame of Jewish passivity in the first extermination action of July 1942.'

As a result of their action, the Polish Home Army provided more weapons, grenades and explosives, although several of the revolvers were found to be defective.

Before the fighting resumed on 16 February, Reichsführer Heinrich Himmler promised Hitler that Warsaw would be *Judenrein* (Jew-free) in time for his 54h birthday on 20 April. It was a promise he was unable to keep.

When the commander of the Warsaw area, SS Oberführer Sammern-Frankenegg, failed to put an end to the fighting, an irate Himmler replaced him with SS Brigadeführer Jürgen Stroop, a veteran of the Eastern Front and a man the Reichsführer could trust to crush an insurrection without mercy.

On 18 April Stroop entered the ghetto with two battalions of Waffen SS, 100 regular soldiers of the Wehrmacht, several units of green-uniformed regular police and up to a hundred members of the Gestapo. Several thousand more troops were held in reserve. In order that the deportations could resume they intended to flush out small groups of 'Jewish bandits' and members of the Polish underground who, they imagined, were arming and training the ghetto fighters.

They were caught by surprise. Rifles cracked from hidden positions in the abandoned buildings and the home-made bombs rained down, sending the battle-hardened soldiers to find cover behind their armoured vehicles, which were set on fire or reversed out of range.

An eyewitness later recalled the chaotic scene as the German soldiers fled for their lives. 'There runs a German soldier shrieking like an insane one, the helmet on his head on fire. Another one shouts madly: "*Juden … Waffen … Juden … Waffen!*" (Jews … weapons!).'

The following day the Germans mounted an all-out assault with heavier armoured support, but they were soon beaten back by rifle and machine gun fire and a firestorm of Molotov cocktails.

Two of the tanks were set on fire and left to burn in the street.

The haul of abandoned guns was a significant and substantial addition to the ghetto armies' arsenal. But the next German attack would see an escalation in the fighting, with the introduction of light artillery which would demolish the buildings that had provided shelter for the Jewish fighters.

Street fighting

The skirmish swiftly became a full-scale battle for every street. As the buildings toppled and burned the Jews were forced to retreat into the basements and underground shelters, where many were buried alive. Members of the Polish underground were moved to offer assistance, firing on Germans outside the ghetto and staging a rescue mission through the sewers to bring 34 Jewish fighters to the so-called Aryan side of the city.

On Easter Sunday, the besieged ghetto fighters received demoralizing news of the capture of a cache of weapons they had been relying on to replenish their dwindling arsenal. The guns they had begun the battle with were already misfiring or seizing up. They hadn't been the best to begin with.

Then on 22 April the Germans brought in flamethrowers.

While the buildings burned and the crack of automatic fire echoed through the deserted streets the sound of a traditional Easter fairground could be heard faintly on the other side of the wall.

Warsaw was going about its business as if nothing untoward or unusual was happening. The congregations crowded into the churches to celebrate Mass and the market stalls did a roaring trade.

Some of Warsaw's citizens sought a vantage point to get a better view of the action. One witness recalls hearing an excited sightseer crying: 'The Jews are frying now! Come and see.'

But the 'untrained street fighters' had demonstrated that their will to survive was unbroken.

On 23 April, the 25-year-old Jewish commander Mordechai Anielewicz made the following journal entry: 'I have a feeling that great things are happening, that what we have undertaken is of tremendous significance.'

A building goes up in flames during the Warsaw uprising.

In the bunkers

Life in the bunkers was harsh and unforgiving. Some had drinking water after digging a makeshift well, while others had to find other sources as their supplies were yellow with rust and undrinkable. The worst part was not knowing what was happening on the outside and when it would be safe to leave the bunker to scavenge for provisions, ammunition and news of friends and family.

Leaving the bunker in daylight was too risky so many were forced to live underground for weeks in the stifling airless shelter. As many as a hundred people including children were confined in the semi-darkness and were under strict orders not to make a sound in case they were heard by the German sappers, who had brought in highly sensitive listening equipment.

In one bunker, it was decided that a newborn baby had to be suffocated because its persistent crying was likely to give away their location. For Jews who put a value on every human life, and prized children above all, this was a sacrifice that traumatized many of the survivors for the rest of their lives.

Their only source of information came from others who managed to scramble through the ruins in search of comrades, or from couriers who came to report on the state of the fighting. Some groups obtained a wireless and listened at the same time every night to the BBC, which broadcast reports on the situation together with messages of support to boost the morale of the besieged fighters. But the wireless had to be used sparingly to avoid the risk of the signal being traced.

As precious as such news was, there was reluctance on the part of the remaining fighters to let anyone enter their subterranean refuge. It was common knowledge that Jewish traitors were being used by the Germans to discover their hiding places. These informants had been coerced or promised their freedom if they betrayed their former comrades and would call out in Hebrew or Yiddish that they had brought food, but few trusted them for they knew there was none to be had in the rubble.

They also knew that even their own people could betray them when tortured or promised that they or their families would be allowed to live.

Over the course of eight weeks, until the official destruction of the ghetto on 16 May 1943, the Jews of Warsaw exacted a terrible cost for every building they were forced to give up and for every one of their own that they had to leave behind unburied in the rubble.

Their stand prompted Nazi Propaganda Minister Goebbels to write in his diary: 'The joke cannot last much longer, but it shows what the Jews are capable of when they have arms in their hands.'

Final days

In the final days of the battle the Germans had brought in poison gas to pump into the basement bunkers and the sewer system, which they also tried to flood until the main pipes were destroyed by a home-made bomb. Survivors spoke of wading waist-deep through the sewers past floating bodies. And without a guide there was no way of knowing where they were in the maze of subterranean tunnels. It was not unknown for them to risk a bullet or worse only to find themselves back where they had started.

But it was the choking smoke from the burning buildings which ultimately drove the survivors to leave their underground bunkers.

'We were beaten by the flames, not the Germans,' said ghetto commander Marek Edelman, the only leader to survive the battle. Even then many walked towards the Germans with their arms up but with guns or grenades concealed in their clenched fists or in their tunics. And died with defiance on their lips.

In response to reports of the uprising the foreign press began to speak in terms of the Jews as worthy allies in a common cause and no longer described them merely as passive victims to be pitied.

'As the British press was the first to admit, the Jews now have a new and different claim for consideration, a claim not of passive victims, but of active allies and partners who have fought the common enemy,' said writer William Zukerman.

And yet, still none of the Allied governments sent aid in any form nor bombed the railway lines that brought thousands to the death camps day after day, week after week.

When the fighting had finally finished and the last dozen Jews had managed to flee through the sewers, there was barely a wall left standing where the ghetto had been. It is estimated that as many as 300 Germans had been killed.

But it had never been a mere question of victory or defeat. In the words of Mordechai Anielewicz: 'It is impossible to put into words what we have been through. What happened exceeded our boldest dreams. The Germans fled twice from the ghetto ... My life's dream has come true. Defence in the ghetto has become a fact.'

The Jews of the Warsaw ghetto had held out for two months, longer than the Polish army in September 1939.

Aftermath

Talking about the demolition of the Great Synagogue, Jürgen Stroop recalled:

'What a marvellous sight it was. A fantastic piece of theatre. My staff and I stood at a distance. I held the electrical device which would detonate all the charges simultaneously. Jesuiter called for silence. I glanced over at my brave officers and men, tired and dirty, silhouetted against the glow of the burning buildings. After prolonging the suspense for a moment, I shouted "Heil Hitler" and pressed the button. With a thunderous, deafening bang and a rainbow burst of colours, the fiery explosion soared towards the clouds, an unforgettable tribute to our triumph over the Jews. The Warsaw ghetto was no more. The will of Adolf Hitler and Heinrich Himmler had been done.'

With the demolition of the Great Synagogue on 16 May 1943 the Germans had carried out a suitably dramatic and highly symbolic final act of destruction for Gross-Aktion Warsaw. But for several weeks after the liquidation of the ghetto on 16 May 1943 hundreds of Jews remained in underground bunkers. Among them were Josef Farber and Zachariah Artstein of the Jewish Fighting Organization, who continued to harass German sappers as they mopped up after the operation.

An enraged Adolf Hitler had ordered the demolition of the ruins, so that not a single wall would be left standing to testify to the ferocity of the Jewish resistance. Prisoners from Auschwitz were brought in to dismantle the remains brick by brick and Polish workers were sent in to demolish the shells of damaged buildings. Unwittingly, it was these men who ended the lives of the last ghetto fighters who were hiding in the basements and bunkers.

Only a dozen or so remained. Injured, exhausted and with no more than a few rounds to fend off their attackers, they had little chance of reaching the Aryan side alive. Several used their last bullets on themselves. A tiny remnant scavenged for scraps in the ruins as the bitter autumn nights set in and managed to inch their way out of the rubble to safety on the Aryan side. Among them were the four survivors from Arieh Neiberg's unit, who had spent more than five months fighting the Germans and enduring great privation.

Residents of the Warsaw ghetto are marched off to the death camps.

Fighting to the end

Arieh Neiberg recalls how he felt at that time:

> 'With the systematic destruction of the remaining buildings
> our possibilities of hiding drastically shrank. Those who were
> in bunkers might one day wake to find themselves buried
> under the rubble of collapsed houses ... Our provisions were
> almost gone, as was our ammunition ... From September we
> were cut off entirely from the Aryan zone, hunted day and
> night by the Germans and cast out, as it were, by our Jewish
> brethren. We became ghosts, nothing less, nothing more.'

Some of the last ghetto fighters were still in hiding in the city
when the Poles staged their own revolt in August 1944 and were
able to fight alongside them to liberate the capital.

Marek Edelman was among them. He later wrote: 'God is
trying to blow out the candle and I'm quickly trying to shield
the flame, taking advantage of His brief inattention. To keep
the flame flickering, even if only for a little while longer than
He would wish.'

Stroop claimed to have exterminated a total of 50,000
inhabitants of the ghetto during the fighting and hundreds of
thousands more were murdered as a result of their transportation
to the death camps, crimes for which he was subsequently
hanged in March 1952. While in prison he admitted that he
had underestimated the courage and determination of his
untrained adversaries.

'The Jews surprised me and my officers [...] with their determination in battle. And believe me, as veterans of World War I and SS members, we knew what determination in battle was all about. The tenacity of your Warsaw Jews took us completely by surprise. That's the real reason the Gross-Aktion lasted as long as it did.'

Ordinary heroes

'Every child saved with my help and the help of all the wonderful secret messengers, who today are no longer living, is the justification of my existence on this earth, and not a title to glory. Heroes do extraordinary things. What I did was not an extraordinary thing. It was normal.

'I was brought up to believe that a person must be rescued when drowning, regardless of religion and nationality. The term "hero" irritates me greatly – the opposite is true – I continue to have pangs of conscience that I did so little.'

Irena Sendler, Polish nurse who helped rescue 2,500 children from the ghetto

Chapter Six

·————————·

GHETTOS IN FLAMES

WARSAW WAS NOT THE ONLY GHETTO THAT refused to surrender to Nazi aggression. There were dozens of lesser-known armed revolts in Lithuania, Czechoslovakia and Russia.

Częstochowa

One hundred and fifty miles (240 km) south-west of Warsaw is the city of Częstochowa, where thousands of Catholics still make the annual pilgrimage to worship the Black Madonna, a 14th century bejewelled icon housed in the Jasna Góra Monastery.

Prior to 1939, almost a quarter of the city's inhabitants were Jews. By the summer of 1942, news of transportations from the Warsaw ghetto reached Częstochowa's 30,000 Jews, who feared they could be next.

Their fears were well founded for on 22 September the Germans began the first of their mass deportations from the city. Members of the nascent Jewish underground (comprising supporters of the Polish Workers' Party and various Zionist groups) retreated into a warren of derelict buildings in the centre of the ghetto and made plans for an armed uprising, although they had few weapons and were initially thinking of setting fire to the ghetto as a symbolic act of martyrdom. One group of youths volunteered to procure the petrol, but hoped to make a final stand and go down fighting. In the following weeks, they reduced their food rations to save money to buy two revolvers.

By the winter of 1942, the 300-strong membership of the Jewish Fighting Organization (ZOB) put themselves under the overall command of Mordecai Zylberberg, who divided them into units of five, so that they could operate independently. Each was assigned a vital task such as digging a tunnel to facilitate the smuggling of goods and people to the outside world, raiding German warehouses to recover confiscated items and procuring German uniforms. In those uniforms resistance fighters could move freely about the city to forage for weapons and couriers could convey messages to the Polish underground. Every task was hazardous and fraught with danger. The procuring of weapons, explosives and ammunition was particularly perilous, for there was no possible justification for having such material in your possession unless you were working for the resistance. A number of valued and experienced operatives died during their hunt for weapons simply because they were caught in the act, or shadowed by informers who had to be silenced on the spot. Often the most carefully made plans had to be abandoned when the unexpected threatened to compromise a mission.

Weapons workshops

Even inside the ghetto the resistance could be caught off guard and forced to improvise. In January 1943, the German police instructed all Jews in the ghetto to assemble in the main square in preparation for deportation. Members of the ZOB fighting group Nadrzeczna 66 were caught up in the round-up and forced to act. Armed with only a single revolver and a knife, they attacked the police and a German officer and were killed. The revolver had jammed and the knife and bare fists were no match for the Germans' weapons. The Germans wasted no time in demonstrating their anger. They dragged 25 of the deportees out of the crowd and shot them there and then.

The deportation went ahead on schedule, with several unarmed members of the resistance being marched to the Polish police headquarters to await transportation. But while they languished in jail, files and other tools were smuggled in to them and with these they later managed to escape from the cattle wagons taking them to an extermination camp. However, few made it all the way back to the ghetto. The Polish police shot several and recaptured the rest.

Routine inspections meant that there was no safe hiding place for weapons, explosives and ammunition and yet these had to be stored somewhere within reach in the event that the Germans ordered the liquidation of the ghetto. So every night the secret weapons workshops were taken to pieces and their components hidden, along with the home-made grenades. And every morning they were reassembled by people who didn't know if this would be the day they had prepared for.

They had no choice but to make their stand in the ghetto as the surrounding forests were patrolled by the Polish Home Army (Armia Krajowa), who would shoot them on sight or hand them over to the Germans. In Koniecpol, a short distance from Częstochowa, a unit of Jewish resistance fighters were lured into a meeting with the local AK, who they assumed to be their compatriots, and were massacred. It was not the only incident of its kind. Several attempts were made by the Częstochowa ghetto underground to contact genuine partisans, but with no success.

Liquidation

In the spring of 1943 they fared better after making contact with the Jewish Fighting Organization in the Warsaw ghetto, from whom they obtained anti-fascist pamphlets and instructions for future actions, but once the Warsaw uprising began in April that source of supply and support was severed. The Częstochowa ghetto was left with a couple of rifles, 18 revolvers and a cache of 30 home-made bombs.

Polish partisans engage Nazi soldiers in a fire fight, 1944.

Further actions often met with failure or forced the Częstochowa fighters to make a futile sacrifice, which was rendered all the more tragic by German reprisals. Dozens of civilians were executed for every operation, whether it claimed German lives or not. Their difficulties were exacerbated by the ever-present risk of betrayal. In such trying times, even Jews could turn against their own.

In June that year, the Częstochowa underground became so desperate that they entrusted a large part of their funds to a German driver, who promised to transport a cache of weapons and three fighters to their comrades in the outlying forests. But before they reached their destination they were ambushed by waiting Gestapo agents and a fierce gun battle ensued. One fighter was killed and another escaped but a third was captured. He was taken to the ghetto where he was tortured in front of his fellow Jews in the certainty that he would name his friends, or that they would come forward to end his ordeal. But he died without betraying anyone.

A short while later on 25 June the Germans marched in to liquidate the ghetto. They sprayed the streets indiscriminately with automatic fire and threw grenades, killing both terrified civilians and members of the resistance.

Surviving members of the underground ran to their designated hiding places and the makeshift arsenal in one of several tunnels, but they were killed before they could organize a defence of the ghetto. Only a handful managed to flee into the forests through one of the tunnels, while those who were the last to break out were surrounded and killed. Hundreds of men, women and children were taken under armed escort to the Jewish cemetery, where they were murdered.

Vilna

'Let us not go like sheep to the slaughter, Jewish youth! Do not believe those who are deceiving you. Out of 80,000 Jews of the Jerusalem of Lithuania (Vilna), only 20,000 remain. In front of your eyes our parents, our brothers and our sisters are being torn away from us. Where are the hundreds of men who were snatched away for labour by the Lithuanian kidnappers? Where are those naked women who were taken away on the horror-night of the provocation? Where are those Jews of the Day of Atonement? And where are our brothers of the second ghetto? Anyone who is taken out through the gates of the ghetto, will never return. All roads of the ghetto lead to Ponary, and Ponary means death. Oh, despairing people – tear

this deception away from your eyes. Your children, your husbands, your wives – are no longer alive – Ponary is not a labour camp. Everyone there is shot. Hitler aimed at destroying the Jews of Europe. It turned out to be the fate of the Jews of Lithuania to be the first. Let us not go like sheep to the slaughter. It is true that we are weak, lacking protection, but the only reply to a murderer is resistance. Brothers, it is better to die as free fighters than to live at the mercy of killers. Resist, resist, to our last breath.'

Abba Kovner, Vilna resistance leader, 1 January 1942

When the Germans liquidated the Vilna ghettos on 23 September 1943 they destroyed more than the lives of the city's 45,000 remaining inhabitants – they erased centuries of a culture that could not be restored merely by returning the survivors to the city that had been known as 'the Jerusalem of Lithuania'. In just over two months from 24 June to 6 September 1941 the Germans executed 35,000 of the city's Jews, leaving just over half of the community to endure the privations of occupation behind the sealed gates of two ghettos which isolated them from their fellow citizens.

If any of Vilna's predominantly Catholic population were inclined to feel sympathy for their former neighbours they were soon cured of that sentiment by the sight of large signs warning them of the danger of contagious disease should they venture beyond the wire.

Within the ghettos, the Jews were reduced to acts of passive

The main entrance to the Vilna ghetto in Lithuania.

resistance and defiance, which took the form of continuing with religious observance in the squalid dwellings they had been forced to crowd into, running makeshift schools and organizing cultural activities to keep the sense of community alive. There were theatre productions and concerts, study groups and social events where they sang and danced as generations before them had done in the shadow of the pogroms.

Various groups met to discuss the perilous situation they found themselves in and to share information gathered by courier from other ghettos, for information was as scarce as fresh bread. The lack of news from the outside world only led to wild unfounded rumours and the fear of what might befall them in the coming hours and days. Others resisted all efforts to make them comply with Nazi edicts and were summarily executed. Some carried out individual acts of sabotage in their workplaces outside the ghetto, to disrupt the German war effort, while a few took direct action on their own initiative.

Words as weapons

In May 1942 three young men defied the ten o'clock curfew to plant a mine on the main railway line. A troop train was derailed and 200 Germans were killed, according to the local farmers who were forced to clear the track the next day. Abraham Sutzkever, author of *Vilna Ghetto*, wrote that the locals managed to conceal some of the weapons in a nearby forest, which were subsequently reclaimed and used by fighters from the ghetto after they escaped.

But no cohesive plan of action was formulated until 23 January 1943 when the Zionist and communist factions formed themselves into a single underground fighting force under the name Fareinkite Partizaner Organizatzie (FPO).

Although the FPO was composed of civilians it was organized along strict military lines with an operation staff, battalion commanders and a central command. Each unit of between three and five fighters was formed from members of the same political party, so that there would be less chance of ideological disagreements. Later this restriction would be abandoned as hatred for the common enemy made ideological and pre-war political affiliations irrelevant.

By that summer, Vilna's underground armoury could boast 50

machine guns, 30 revolvers, dozens of grenades and thousands of rounds of ammunition, much of it smuggled out of the German ammunition factory where several members of the FPO were working as slave labour.

The underground's main weapon, however, was hard news – unvarnished reports of the Nazis' latest defeats on the Russian front – to counter the relentless barrage of propaganda forced upon the occupied nations by Joseph Goebbels' Ministry of Propaganda and Enlightenment. Since listening to foreign radio broadcasts was forbidden under threat of death, this information was circulated by an underground newspaper, the *Flag of Freedom*, printed in a secret workshop outside the ghetto and distributed to the general population. A Russian-language pamphlet was also printed for the Soviet POWs and a Yiddish language summary was handwritten for those inside the ghetto.

Ultimatum

Successful armed resistance, however, requires more than the obtaining of weapons. It must be matched with the will to fight back regardless of the consequences and that will appeared to be lacking when the crisis came.

On 16 July the Gestapo learned the identity of the leader of the Vilna ghetto underground after torturing two of his communist comrades and demanded that the ghetto police hand him over. Isaac Witenberg was duly arrested, but as he was being taken to the main gate his guards were overpowered by members of the underground and he disappeared into a warren of alleys and side streets. Within hours, the German authorities issued an ultimatum. Witenberg was to be handed over to them by daybreak or they would liquidate the ghetto.

But while the FPO were ready and willing to defy the Germans, the ghetto's inhabitants were not. They made it clear to their representatives that they were not prepared to die for one of their leaders and that he must be surrendered to save the women and children. The FPO had no option but to find Witenberg and order him to give himself up. He refused and argued that the Germans wanted to kill the resistance leaders as a prelude to transporting the inhabitants and razing the ghetto to the ground. But he was finally worn down by their insistence and walked out under guard to a waiting Gestapo car. The ghetto police made a show of escorting him to the gate with their weapons in their hands as if they were complying with their orders, but it was Witenberg's decision alone.

The following day news reached the ghetto that their former leader was dead. Whether he died by his own hand after swallowing a phial of poison that he was believed to have been given or whether his interrogators beat him to death is not known. But the repercussions of this distressing episode were fatally divisive. The FPO lost the support of the community and decided that they would be better relocating to the woods outside the city. Tragically, many of them were murdered there by the Germans. Only a dozen or so survived to form the core of a new partisan unit which eventually numbered close to 400.

FPO driven out

German reprisals for the flight of those murdered fighters in the forest were swift and merciless. Members of their families were rounded up and Jews from the work camps who had joined the FPO en route to the forest were executed. Eighty were killed in all, along with a German NCO who had been transporting FPO fighters in his truck and hiding them in his own house.

The discovery that one of their own had been aiding the Jews appears to have triggered the order to move in on the ghetto on 1 September. Barricades were set up by the FPO who defended their positions as best they could against overwhelming odds, but the lack of ammunition forced some to surrender, leaving the remaining group to negotiate a withdrawal to save the ghetto from total destruction. The Germans agreed and during the lull in the fighting 200 resistance fighters escaped to the Narocz and Rudnitsky forests to continue the fight.

A number chose to remain and defend the ghetto when the Germans returned to continue the deportations they had begun in the first week of September. At that time 8,000 of Vilna's Jews were transported to slave labour camps in Estonia, many to toil in the oil shale mines. But when the Germans saw that the FPO still had sufficient men and women to defend the ghetto they withdrew and reassigned their men to the hunt for partisans in the surrounding forests.

However, the stalemate could not be allowed to continue, for the Germans had a quota to fulfil. On 23 and 24 September they entered the ghetto in force with 200 Ukrainians and drove the surviving FPO members out through the sewers. Many ghetto fighters were killed in the escape attempt while others were captured and executed in full view of those they had hoped to save. The next day the remaining inhabitants of the Vilna ghetto were transported to the Vaivara concentration camp in Estonia. A very fortunate few were transferred to the Heereskraftpark labour camp, where they were protected by Wehrmacht Major Karl Plagge and the men under his command. Shortly before the SS were expected to assume command of the camp Plagge warned his Jewish slave workers, who went into hiding. As a result an estimated 250 survived the war.

Minsk

The Minsk ghetto, which was established on 25 July 1941, was seen as a prison by its Jewish population, but it served as a sanctuary for non-Jewish Byelorussian resistance fighters who were in hiding from the Gestapo. Nearly two dozen wounded partisans were smuggled into the ghetto during the German occupation, where they received treatment in the ghetto hospital and false papers giving them new temporary identities. These were thought necessary in case the Jewish police queried the presence of the new arrivals, as the Germans rarely inspected the wards for fear of contracting typhus.

The ghetto contributed 10,000 Jewish partisans to the war effort, the largest number of any ghetto in Eastern Europe. They were trained and armed inside the ghetto so that they would be ready to fight the moment they joined the partisans in the countryside.

But when the Germans forced the Byelorussian partisans further into the hinterland it became more difficult to contact them, so the ghetto fighters found themselves forming all-Jewish units. Five thousand of these fighters were killed during operations which included the derailment of German troop and supply trains, attacks on military convoys and the disruption of communications. But the action which gave the ghetto's inhabitants the grimmest satisfaction was the assassination of Generalkommissar Wilhelm Kube.

In March 1942 Kube had commanded the execution squad which murdered all of the children in the ghetto's children's home by burying them alive. While the children screamed he is said to have stood by and thrown sweets into the pit. His assassination was more than an act of defiance or even revenge. It was a signal to the Nazis and their Byelorussian collaborators that there were those who would willingly sacrifice themselves to seek retribution for such atrocities.

As there was no hope of a man getting close enough to kill Kube, the Jewish deputy commander of the partisans entrusted a woman with the mission. Halina Mazanik was a servant in the house which Kube had commandeered. She slipped a time bomb under his bed which a female courier had brought earlier that day, then she left the house for the safety of the forest where she and her family were being hidden by the partisans.

Sabotage

Almost every able-bodied person in the ghetto played their part. Those who worked outside the ghetto in the German-owned

Wilhelm Kube was assassinated by his servant, who had been recruited by local Jewish partisans.

factories and workshops disrupted production and deliberately ruined their work, although to do so meant certain death for them and their fellow workers if they were discovered. Stealing weapon parts from the repair shops also brought instant and merciless retribution, but it was often the only thing that gave them hope. Many had resigned themselves to the belief that it was only a matter of time before the ghetto would be razed to the ground and they would be massacred or transported to their death in Sobibór. And so they took a pride in the damage they could inflict on their persecutors, even if it meant spoiling consignments of leather boots with a corrosive chemical manufactured in the ghetto's own underground laboratory or poisoning a shipment of alcohol assigned for the Eastern Front.

In Minsk, the *Judenrat* were pro-partisan to a man. So when the Germans ordered them to confiscate clothes or other items from the ghetto inhabitants for the Wehrmacht or German settlers in the east, the *Judenrat* would give a share to the partisans, who were as much in need of warm clothing and basic necessities as the ghetto's inmates.

But when the Germans learned that the *Judenrat* were co-operating with the underground, they executed every member but one as a warning to those who would aid the resistance. In spite of the constant danger, the underground would not be intimidated even when one of their female couriers was tortured by the Gestapo, who demanded to know where a particular partisan was hiding. She was shot for refusing to tell them and so was her five-year-old daughter, together with all 70 inhabitants of the house she had been living in.

Deceiving the Gestapo

The Gestapo then issued an ultimatum, threatening to execute every member of the *Judenrat* and liquidate part of the ghetto if the wanted man was not given up. The Jewish leadership did not have enough weapons to stage an uprising, but they were quick-witted. The chairman of the *Judenrat* made a copy of the wanted man's identification papers then soaked it in the blood of one of the men executed the previous night. He handed it to the Gestapo claiming that he had found it on one of the bodies. They accepted it as proof of his death and withdrew from the ghetto.

Even the Nazis who officially considered all Jews to be '*Untermenschen*' (subhumans) were forced to admit they were dealing with an uncommonly resourceful adversary. According to a military report sent to the Reichskommissar for Riga dated 20 November 1941 the Nazis believed that the Jews were 'far superior' in intelligence to the 'mass of the White Russian populace'. The Jews had been identified as 'the driving force of the resistance movement' and were found to be 'the originators and instigators and in most instances even the perpetrators'.

Bialystok

The 50,000 Jewish men, women and children crammed into the Bialystok ghetto in north-eastern Poland in August 1941 did not consider themselves fortunate, even though they had survived the massacres that followed the German occupation of the city on 27 June. Two thousand had been shot in the streets and hundreds more were burned alive in the main synagogue that day. A week later, 200 more were executed in the fields outside the city boundary and on 12 July a further 5,000 were murdered on the same site. But the Nazis were not satisfied with liquidating their enemies. They wanted to see them humiliated and shamed. And so on 30 July thousands were paraded through the streets to the Jewish cemetery, where they were forced to desecrate the graves and smash the statues of Marx, Engels, Lenin and Stalin.

That September, 4,000 Jews were transported to the ghetto at Pruzhany and from there to Auschwitz in January 1943. Many more would have followed had the German authorities not required them to man the factories and workshops supplying the SS and the Wehrmacht in Russia, a policy which also profited the Nazi businessmen who had Aryanized those industries. The *Judenrat* in Bialystok were quick to gauge their usefulness to their Nazi overseers and determined to ensure the survival of the ghetto's inhabitants by maintaining production and discouraging sabotage. As a consequence, Bialystok's Jewish community were spared the dreaded round-ups and deportations and were able to move freely around the city and smuggle extra rations into the ghetto on their return.

Judenrat *collusion*

Incredibly, the Jewish underground movement urged their own people to share their meagre rations, clothing and

Jews wait for selection on the platform at Birkenau station: those deemed fit for work were sent to be registered; the others were sent to the gas chambers.

medical supplies with Russian POWS who were suffering privation in camps outside the city. The head of the *Judenrat* in Bialystok, Ephraim Barasz, did not collude with the Germans out of fear, nor did he profit from his position, but nevertheless he was seen as a collaborator by the resistance, who believed it was the duty of every Jew to deny the Nazis their skills and their labour.

But even within the underground there was dissent and disagreement as to how best to resist the occupation, with some factions refusing to co-operate with any group affiliated with the *Judenrat* and others opposing violence while the ghetto was operating as a 'model' and deportations were seemingly suspended. The ghetto was seen by various of its own inhabitants as a refuge of sorts, for the city was bordered in the west by vast impenetrable forests patrolled by Polish partisans who would kill Jews as readily as they would the Nazis. To the north, south and east, the country was largely under the control of

Soviet partisans, who could be considered allies in the fight against fascism. But the Jews of Bialystok could never be certain who they could trust or whether they would have any allies or have to rely on their own resources when the Germans moved in.

Weapons shortage

It was only after the death of one of the more intransigent resistance leaders in July 1943 that the various factions set their differences aside for the common good and adopted the name Anti-Fascist Bloc. And just in time, for the Bialystok ghetto was designated for liquidation just four weeks later.

But they would receive no assistance from the Polish Home Army, whose commanders in exile had grave doubts regarding the political allegiance of Polish Jews. Repeated pleas for arms were rejected by the Polish leadership in London, in the belief that the Jews would side with the Soviets. Appeals to the Polish underground were also in vain. Its leaders sympathized with the ghetto fighters but had few weapons to spare. It was a desperate situation and an urgent one. Any day the Germans might encircle the ghetto and the inhabitants would be cut off from the outside world.

The last days of July and early August were particularly fraught as the Bialystok underground made contact with local peasants who were known to have scavenged the countryside for weapons abandoned by retreating Polish soldiers in the early months of the war. Dealing with these people proved as risky as stealing guns from the German barracks, but the women and children shared the risk for it was they who smuggled the stolen arms into the ghetto.

For all the danger they put themselves in the reward was pretty slight. On the eve of the planned uprising on 15 August 1943, their arsenal comprised two dozen rifles, one heavy machine gun, several sub-machine guns and a hundred hand-guns. Many of these were in poor condition and seized after firing a round or two. That day *Judenrat* leader Ephraim Barasz was informed that the 40,000 inhabitants of the ghetto would be deported to Lublin the following day as they were no longer of economic value to the Reich.

But they would not go meekly to their deaths as many of their race had done before. As one of them put it:

'What have we got to lose?'

Though outnumbered and outgunned, the 500 men and women of the Bialystok resistance were determined to die with dignity and take as many of their murderers with them as they could. That morning they posted their defiance on the walls of the ghetto.

'Five million European Jews have already been murdered by Hitler and his executioners ... Each of us is under a sentence of death and we have nothing to lose! ... Let us not behave like sheep going to the slaughter!'

The Germans were also resolved not to underestimate the opposition as their comrades had done in Warsaw some months before. They marched into the ghetto with three battalions, two of them composed of the dreaded Galician Ukrainians, whose reputation for pitiless cruelty preceded them. These were augmented by dozens of German and auxiliary police, who sealed off the ghetto while the troops moved in armed with machine guns and artillery, supported by armoured cars and tanks. Before the resistance could take up defensive positions they were being corralled into three narrow streets backing on to the perimeter fence.

Time and again they rushed the fence but were beaten back while the elderly, women and children advanced on the Ukrainian troops and were mowed down and bayoneted, sacrificing themselves to give the fighters time to make a breach in the perimeter. For six days, the unequal struggle went on until the ghetto workers set their factories and workshops ablaze. In the carnage and confusion, many were able to break out and join the partisans, who had been prevented from joining the fight by the German troops who had been sent to seal off the forests.

As the Polish writer and Second World War veteran Reuben Ainsztein notes in *Jewish Resistance in Nazi-Occupied Eastern Europe*, had they only had one load in ten of the arms dropped by the RAF for the Polish underground, 'the fighters of the Bialystok ghetto would have made their murderers pay a fairer price for the 40,000 lives they attempted to defend'.

The two Lubas

On 16 August 1943 12-year-old Luba Olenski was among thousands of Jews herded on to a cattle truck bound for Treblinka after the Nazis liquidated the Bialystok ghetto. She was the only surviving member of her family and for the past two years had been sheltered by distant relatives in the squalor of the overcrowded hovel they were forced to share with several other families.

No one on the train that night entertained any illusions of what awaited them at their destination. Their only thought must have been how to survive the long hours of that final agonizing journey without food, water or fresh air.

There was no chance to escape and yet at some point one of Luba's companions saw an opportunity and urged the others to follow. Luba was among five who managed to jump from the moving train as it sped through the Polish countryside. The others scattered in different directions, leaving the teenager to wander alone for weeks, fearful and starving.

By chance Luba eventually came upon a group of Jewish partisans, who were living in underground bunkers deep in Bryansk forest. They were the Olenski partisans, led by David Olenski whom Luba would marry when their ordeal was behind them. Among their number was a young woman who was also named Luba – Luba Wrobel – who was then 20 years old and a veteran of the resistance. She had been one of the few to escape from the Sokoly ghetto. The two young women became friends and slept under the same blanket at night, more for safety than for warmth, for they no longer trusted anyone, not even their comrades in the forest.

The two young women were among hundreds of female Jewish resistance fighters who it is estimated comprised about 10 per cent of the Jewish partisans. Many provided medical care or acted as couriers, but there were others who took an active part in raids and military missions: women such as Sarah Fortis, who formed an all-female partisan unit in Greece, and Eta Wrobel in Poland.

Luba Olenski would live to write an account of her experiences, but the names and fate of the others might have remained unknown had it not been for Jewish partisan photographer Faye Schulman.

Schulman survived the murder of her family and 1,850 other inhabitants of the Lenin ghetto in August 1942 because the Nazis knew she was a photographer and wanted a visual record of their murderous '*Aktions*'. It was only after printing the pictures she had taken of a mass grave that she recognized members of her own family among the bodies. Once she escaped into the forest, she devoted her talent to recording the activities and precarious life of the partisans. As she later said:

'I want people to know that there was resistance. Jews did not go like sheep to the slaughter. Many fought back — if there was the slightest opportunity — and thousands lost their lives fighting the enemy and working to save lives. I was a photographer. I have pictures. I have proof.'

Fight to the death

Similar stories can be told of other ghettos. In Lachwa in south-west Byelorussia on 3 August 1942 the 2,000-strong population of the ghetto watched in stunned silence as truckloads of SS sat down to eat in the field outside the ghetto. They had spent the morning murdering tens of thousands of men, women and children in nearby Hohorodek and Luniniece. When asked by a representative of the *Judenrat* what they were doing there, an SS officer replied that they had come to liquidate the ghetto, but that they would spare the members of the *Judenrat*, the camp doctor and 30 or so others who might be of use to the Reich.

At that, the inhabitants set fire to their own houses and snatched up whatever weapons came to hand. With hammers and axes, they attacked their would-be murderers, killing several as they fired into the crowd. About 1,400 of Lachwa's Jews were massacred that morning, but almost 600 managed to break through the ghetto gates and run for the cover of the woods. Many were subsequently killed there by the pursuing SS and local Nazi sympathizers, but 120 survived to join the partisans in the region's Chobot forest. Their main aim was to avenge the deaths of their friends and families.

A similar scene occurred in the small town of Tuczyn near Rovno in Ukraine, where the ghetto's inhabitants had been forced to appeal to the Gestapo for protection after the locals massacred 70 of their number including women and children. They were told that the killing of Jews was the exclusive right of the German occupying forces and the matter would be investigated.

Tuczyn

On 23 September 1942, the Germans and their Ukrainian collaborators surrounded the Tuczyn ghetto and ordered the inhabitants to assemble at the main gate for transportation to work camps. The population were under no illusions as to what this meant as they had been forewarned by the recent influx of Jewish refugees from neighbouring towns, who had witnessed atrocities first hand. These frightened and desperate people had swollen the population of the Tuczyn ghetto to 3,000 souls, all of them now crowded into three narrow streets.

Defying the German command, they set fire to their wooden houses and stormed the main gate, lashing out at the soldiers with improvised weapons, while those who were armed with guns and grenades took their toll on the stupefied Germans, who had not expected to meet armed resistance. Two thousand of the ghetto's inhabitants breached the ghetto fence and found refuge in the forests, leaving behind dozens of dead and wounded Germans and Ukrainians.

But life on the run brought its own problems. A few found work with the local farmers, but many were eventually worn down by hunger, lack of shelter and the constant threat posed by local peasants, who harassed and hunted them at every opportunity. Four hundred survivors were reluctantly driven back to the ruins of the ghetto, persuaded by the promise of leniency and rumours that those who had been caught had not been shot but had been returned to the charred remains of the ghetto. They were all executed, as were another 150 who were encouraged to return that winter.

Such incidents in remote and isolated towns might have remained unknown were it not for the willingness of the survivors to relive their harrowing experiences and the co-operation of a few of the locals who were prepared to talk about what they had witnessed during the war.

Chapter Seven

REVOLT!

UNDERGROUND RESISTANCE GROUPS WERE FORMED IN SEVERAL concentration and forced labour camps including Lublin, Dachau and Buchenwald while armed revolts were organized in three of the extermination camps – Sobibór, Treblinka and Auschwitz. Although hundreds escaped from Sobibór and Treblinka, those who dynamited the crematoria at Auschwitz did so knowing that they had no hope of escape.

The fear of silence

One of the most persistently asked questions regarding the Holocaust is why the Jews did not resist on their arrival at the camps.

The answer is that while many had no idea of what awaited them, those who suspected the worst were so carefully controlled by the guards that they had no opportunity to resist.

Auschwitz survivor Rudolf Vrba suggests another possibility.

Vrba worked on the ramp, the station platform where new arrivals were herded through the selection process.

He personally witnessed the processing of some 300 transports over a period of about eight months, a procedure he described as 'the greatest confidence trick the world has ever known'.

It was, he said, simple and effective.

'As soon as a transport arrived it was surrounded with SS men with sub-machine guns, rifles or heavy bamboo canes. As the dazed victims tumbled out, they were forbidden to speak and about 20 or 30 SS men were detailed to ensure that this rule was observed.'

The new arrivals were 'thoroughly confused', disorientated and 'demoralized by the fetid squalor' they had endured for many days in the sealed cattle wagons. He could see that they were unlikely to give trouble because they had their families with them and could see how the SS treated those who protested. 'Without speech, without a whisper to fan spirit into flame, there can be no rebellion.'

The appearance of a Red Cross ambulance may have given them hope that the brutal 'excesses' of their oppressors might be constrained, but it was yet another Nazi deception. For it was carrying the canisters of Zyklon-B industrial insecticide that would be used to kill them within the hour.

Sobibór

The three barbed wire fences that surrounded Sobibór extermination camp were ten feet (three metres) high. On the other side was a mined perimeter, a deep flooded trench and a fourth outer fence, also of barbed wire and of the same unscalable height. A network of guard towers and searchlights ensured that every foot of the camp was under the vigilant eye of the SS day and night.

Inside the compound armed Ukrainian auxiliaries herded the new prisoners off the trains and through the selection process, taunting them, beating the stragglers and generally demonstrating their zeal for their work to the amusement of their SS overseers.

Those prisoners who had been spared the gas chambers during the selection process were put to work and fed just enough to keep them from dying before they had served their purpose. Tens of thousands died from starvation, dehydration, disease, exhaustion and the systematic, unrelieved brutality that broke their spirit long before it broke their bodies.

There was no escape from Sobibór and of those who still lived in hope of doing so, few had the strength to attempt it. Some had tried and were shot before they reached the wire.

Retribution was swift and pitiless. After a married couple had been killed while attempting to escape, 150 prisoners in their block were taken out and shot. Their murder was not intended as a deterrent but as revenge for an act of defiance. Punishment for daring to disobey their Nazi masters was sadistic and medieval in its theatrical cruelty. When 70 Dutch Jews tried to escape by bribing a guard, they were decapitated. Lesser offences were punished with a bullwhip that would reduce the toughest man to a whimpering child. And if the victim begged them to stop, they would start the prescribed number of lashes all over again.

Arrival

Under such a regime it was inevitable that some of the prisoners would choose to attempt to escape, even if it meant certain death. At least they would die as men.

The historic revolt at Sobibór on 14 October 1943, during which 600 prisoners managed to break out of the camp, was led by 33-year-old Russian POW Alexander Pechersky. Pechersky was a Jewish junior officer in the Soviet army who at the time of his capture had managed to hide the fact that he was suffering from typhus, a contagious disease which the Germans sought to 'cure' by killing all those infected with it.

He had arrived at what he took to be a deserted railway station after a five-day journey in a cattle wagon with 70 Jewish men, women and children from the Minsk ghetto. Conditions were appalling. It was so crowded that he was forced to endure much of the journey standing up and without sleep as there was no space to lie down or even sit. They had been denied food, water and even a stop to allow them 'to perform their natural functions'.

At their destination they were shunted into a siding where they were given water but no food and locked in the wagon for a fifth night. Through an opening strung with barbed wire

Pechersky could see a forest to one side and a barbed wire fence on the other, with the name of the station in Gothic script – 'Sobibór'.

When they were finally allowed out the next morning their first sight of the camp was a white cottage behind barbed wire, out of which emerged a group of German officers with whips in their hands. One of them ordered all the unmarried men who were cabinetmakers or carpenters to step aside. About 80 POWS stepped forward, including Pechersky. They were taken to a block furnished with bare wooden bunk beds and little else. They never saw the women and children again.

Witness to barbarity

Shortly after their arrival Pechersky saw smoke rising in the middle distance and smelt a strong acrid odour. He was told it was from the burning of his comrades' bodies, the men who had come with him on the train. 'Every other day a transport of 2,000 arrives here and the camp has been in existence for nearly a year and a half. So figure it out for yourself.' The man who told him this was one of the men who sorted out the clothes of those who had been herded into the gas chambers. He saw the 'process' first hand and was under no illusions that he would be next in line for 'the baths' when his usefulness had come to an end.

That first night Pechersky could not sleep, although he was exhausted from the journey. When he closed his eyes all he saw was the face of a little girl with curly hair who had been with them on the train. Her fate was too dreadful to contemplate.

Soon after their arrival he began to keep a diary in a deliberately distorted hand, so it could not be read by anyone else if it was discovered. It made for distressing reading. The cruelty of the guards and their Ukrainian auxiliaries is recorded in all its hideous barbarity. But as a historic document it is unique in that it appears to have been the only first-hand account of the Sobibór revolt.

The break-out had been planned by Pechersky and six comrades from the Minsk transport who, shortly after their arrival, made contact with a pre-existing underground group of 20 Czech, German, French and Polish Jews. The latter provided vital information regarding the guards' routine and other important details that would prove crucial to the success of the revolt.

It began with the execution of 18 inmates who had been sick for days and were therefore of no use to the Germans. The wife of one of the men took his arm as he was too weak to walk and went with him to share his fate rather than live on without him. Such scenes were an almost daily occurrence. There was no single inciting incident, but a steady wearing down until the prisoners saw no alternative but armed revolt.

Planning the revolt

The plan was to kill the German officers swiftly and silently, one at a time, before their absence aroused suspicion. This was vital to the success of the break-out, and so it was assigned to the Soviet POWs that Pechersky knew he could trust. One moment of hesitation or failure 'and we're all done for', he told them.

At 3.30 pm a Kapo (trustee or overseer) would find an excuse to go to Camp II with the three Soviet prisoners, who were to kill the first four German officers by enticing them into the building one at a time. No one would be allowed to leave the camp during this phase of the operation and if any prisoner should make a scene or interfere they were to be silenced.

At 4 pm the telephone lines connecting Camp II to the reserve guard barracks were to be cut and the wires hidden so as to delay any attempt at repairs. At the same time the guards in the main camp would be enticed into the workshops on some pretext and killed by two men assigned to the task, who would then take their pistols.

At 4.30 the inmates would line up and march towards the main gates as if they were going on a work detail. Those at the front of the column would break off to attack the arsenal while the rest marched on to cover the attack. With the weapons taken from the arsenal the armed prisoners would then kill the guards at the main gate and the watchtower.

If the plan failed for any reason they had an alternative, which was equally treacherous. They would storm the barbed wire fence behind the officers' villa, which some would hack through while others threw stones at the strip of land beyond the wire. This would explode the mines. They would then cut through the outer wire and make a break for the woods beyond.

But the day before the break-out there were crucial questions to answer. Little was left to chance. Pechersky had noticed that the guards on the watchtower always gave their ammunition to those who relieved them, which suggested that the relief guards carried unloaded weapons. To confirm this he arranged to visit the guards' barracks, where he pretended to carry out repairs to the doors while sneaking a look at the rifles and magazines. Both were empty as he had expected.

Mass break-out

That night the decision was made to attempt the break-out the following day. Knives and makeshift hatchets were distributed, but only the leaders were privy to their plans. Even the prisoners could not trust each other after the treatment they had suffered. Escapes had been thwarted before because of the promise of extra rations.

But even the best-laid plans can be derailed by the unexpected and it was almost so in Sobibór. One of the prisoners aroused the suspicion of a guard by dressing in his best suit as he had no other civilian clothes. The guard took him away and this meant they lost one of the key men who had been assigned to take the Soviet POWs to Camp II. Pechersky had no option but to give that role to another man.

The assassinations went without a hitch but one of the targets, the sadistic head of the camp administration, did not come to inspect the workshop at the appointed time. The decision was made to go ahead with the escape anyway. His day would have to come at some other time in some other place.

The film Escape from Sobibor *commemorated the efforts of Alexander Pechersky and 600 fellow inmates who overcame the odds to escape the notorious death camp.*

At the shrill sound of a whistle prisoners began streaming out into the parade ground and surging towards the main gate. It had been wise to keep the break-out secret but now there was confusion and commotion, which threatened to disrupt the orderly march to the main gate. The plan had been to fool the guards into thinking it was merely a work detail on the move, but now it looked like a mass panic, with people screaming and jostling for fear they might be left behind. In all, 600 wretchedly thin, brutalized and frantic prisoners from half a dozen occupied countries descended on the perimeter. In the stampede, the guards were mown down and killed and the sheer force of bodies broke through the main gate and headed for the woods. The attack on the arsenal had failed as the guards, alerted by the noise, opened fire with automatic weapons.

Don't look back

Prisoners fell in every direction, including many of those who stormed the wire to the left of the main gate and then ran the gauntlet of the minefield. In the midst of this confusion Pechersky kept his head and made for the wire behind the officers' villa and the strip of land beyond, which he correctly suspected was not mined. Three of his companions were killed within sight of the wire, but Pechersky made it clear of the compound and ran breathless to the woods, while bullets ripped into the ground around him and felled those who followed behind.

A heady mixture of fear and adrenaline coursed through his emaciated body, urging him to run faster. It gave him an energy he didn't know he possessed. And perhaps hope, too, spurred him on as he neared the trees. Not until he reached the cover of the woods did he pause to look back. He saw his companions running with their heads down and backs bent in the hope that they might dodge the ceaseless stream of bullets. Many were lucky and made it to the trees where they hurriedly formed into small groups before heading for the open country beyond. But there were so many bodies twisted into obscene shapes on the wire, in the minefield and on the open ground where they made an easy target for the sentries. There could be no sense of elation for those who made it, only relief mixed with a numbing horror of what they had witnessed that day and in the months and years that had preceded it.

Hunted

It had been agreed that if they were successful each group would venture in a different direction: the Polish Jews would head west where their knowledge of the language might improve their chances of evading capture; the Russians journeyed east; while the Western Europeans (the Dutch, French and Germans) were at a loss as to where to hide. None of those who survived the break-out could return home. Many joined up with the partisans, but the rest had no idea where to go or what to do. With the exception of the Russian POWs very few were soldiers and so had no military or survival training. They also had no forged travel documents, money or contacts, so they had no hope of linking up with an underground organization that could pass them on to someone who could smuggle them to a neutral country. They had only each other and were in a wretched state.

Many were cadaverously thin and weak and others were sick with typhus and would eventually die from the disease, deprived as they were of the medicines which might have cured them.

Of the 600 inmates who attempted to escape that day it is believed that about 200 were shot before they reached the wire and another 200 did not make it through the minefield.

Of the 200 or so who scattered across the countryside, dozens were hunted down and shot by the SS and German troops in the days and weeks that followed the break-out. At one point the Luftwaffe were brought into the pursuit to strafe small groups who had been spotted in open country. Those who evaded the Germans found themselves prey to the Polish Home Army and zealous locals who were eager to join the hunt. More might have been murdered had it not been for a courageous Polish worker at the Chelm telegraph office, who had deliberately delayed passing on an 'urgent' call for reinforcements.

Erasing the evidence

In the end, just over 100 escapees are believed to have survived, including the 60 men and women in Pechersky's group who eventually made contact with the Russian partisans. (Pechersky lived to serve as the chief prosecution witness at the 1962 Soviet trial of 11 Ukrainian guards, all of whom were found guilty of the crimes committed at Sobibór.)

Fewer than a dozen Germans had died in the break-out. However, 38 Ukrainian guards had been either killed or wounded and 40 more had fled for fear of what their Nazi masters might do in retaliation for their failure to crush the revolt.

But far more significant was the loss of face suffered by the Nazis. Six hundred 'racially inferior' and poorly armed prisoners, seen as *Untermenschen*, had overwhelmed and outwitted their guards and more than 100 were now free. These were referred to as 'rebels' in subsequent communiqués, as the Germans could not risk it becoming common knowledge that they had allowed Jews to escape. Just two days after the revolt an enraged Reichsführer Himmler ordered all traces of the camp to be obliterated. The crematoria and watchtowers were dynamited, the barracks demolished and the ten-foot (three-metre) high barbed wire fences were pulled down and dismantled. The transports continued to roll elsewhere in the east, but the gas chambers of Sobibór were silenced.

More than 600,000 Jews had perished in the camp, but after 14 October 1943 not a single life would be added to that figure.

When the Soviet forces raised the red flag over the Reichstag on 2 May 1945 Semyon Rozenfeld, a 23-year-old former inmate of Sobibór, scratched three words into the bullet-riddled wall, the first being the name of his home town in Byelorussia where his long journey had begun – 'Baranowicze-Sobibór-Berlin'.

Treblinka

Many stories of individual acts of defiance and armed resistance to Nazi oppression will never be known, while some have come to light by the merest chance.

One such account was that of the attempted uprising at Treblinka extermination camp, 80 km (50 miles) north-east of Warsaw in early August 1943, two months before the break-out was attempted at Sobibór.

It had been documented in the diary belonging to one of the ten men who organized the Treblinka rising and was found in the jacket he abandoned on his arrival at Sobibór. Its discovery was extremely fortuitous for the organizers of the Sobibór revolt as it documented the measures the Germans had recently implemented to prevent a similar uprising happening in other camps. Its writer went to the gas chambers not knowing the part his diary would play in the comparative success of the Sobibór revolt.

The anonymous writer described how the inmates had

managed to make a copy of the key to the ammunition store by pouring sand into the lock so that the Germans would take it to the Jewish locksmith to make a new one. From the mould he made, a second key was cut which gave them access to the ammunition. But such a simple task, which would have been completed in less than an hour under normal conditions, took a painstaking four months without the proper tools. Frequently it had to be halted to avoid the prying eyes of informers.

Death camp

Treblinka had originally been built as a slave labour camp, but by the summer of 1942 it had been adapted to serve as an extermination camp, primarily to liquidate more than a quarter of a million inhabitants of the Warsaw ghetto. By the time the gas chambers and crematoria were dismantled by the Germans in October 1943, an estimated 800,000 Jews had died there, making it the second-largest death camp next to Auschwitz.

One of the few survivors of the Treblinka uprising was Samuel Rajzman, whose experiences of Treblinka were written down and smuggled out of Poland in the closing months of the war. They were read by the US House Committee on Foreign Affairs, which was then debating the fate of Nazi war criminals. The following year Rajzman appeared in person at the Nuremberg Trials.

In Treblinka in the spring of 1943 he had been among the few prisoners at the heart of the 'conspiratorial committee', who planned to set fire to the camp and sabotage 'the cruellest engines' devised for their destruction. But without weapons they knew they had no hope of success. They had obtained a few that had been smuggled in by survivors of the Warsaw ghetto, from whom they also found the courage to stage their own revolt. But if they were to have any chance of overwhelming their German and Ukrainian guards and blasting a way through the barbed wire, they would have to obtain a quantity of rifles and explosives.

Consequently their thoughts turned to devising a way of breaking into the armoury. They would then need to organize three 'combat units' to lead the assault and clear the way for the majority of the 700 prisoners who would be unarmed. But even after obtaining a copy of the key their carefully laid plans were ruined by a cruel twist of fate. Their leader, a Polish army officer, was provoked into attacking a German Untersturmführer and before he could be captured he took his own life.

Weapons heist

The loss of their leader was a severe blow to the prisoners' morale. No one else felt qualified to take charge or to take responsibility for the failure of the uprising, which they knew had little chance of success. It was likely to be a suicide mission and no one wanted to die for nothing. Even at this lowest point, they were only willing to sacrifice themselves so long as there was a chance that it would not be in vain.

Fortunately, only a fortnight later another former Polish army officer, Dr Leichert, was brought into the camp and after being told of the planned revolt he agreed to be their leader.

But for three long anxious months they had to wait for an

opportunity to enter the armoury and remove as many weapons as possible without arousing suspicion.

On 2 August, a group of prisoners was ordered to work near the armoury, which provided the cover and distraction they needed. Using the duplicate key, they let one of their group inside then locked the door behind him. At the same time another prisoner was sent to the guard room adjoining the armoury to divert the guard while others cut a pane of glass from a window at the rear of the building. Through this opening the weapons would be passed to a waiting cart. If the Germans asked what the cart was doing so close to the armoury, they would be told that it was needed to clear a pile of debris nearby. But none of the guards showed any interest and within minutes 20 rifles and the same number of grenades were loaded on to the cart along with a number of revolvers and a large quantity of ammunition.

Up in flames

While the arms were being distributed, other preparations were being made. The group had acquired cans of petrol from a prisoner who worked in the camp garage and this had been substituted for the disinfectant that was routinely sprayed around the buildings in a vain attempt to prevent the spread of infection. It was a wonder the Germans did not detect the smell of petrol as it was sprayed liberally around strategic buildings that morning, but either they assumed it was being used instead of disinfectant or they simply didn't smell it through the pungent stench of decay and the pervasive smoke from the crematoria.

At precisely 3.45 a single rifle shot signalled the start of the revolt. It was followed by a series of explosions as the grenades were thrown at the buildings that had been soaked in petrol.

The fire quickly spread throughout the camp and consumed all of the main buildings including the barracks, the prisoners' blocks and the storerooms. All went up in flames with the exception of the gas chambers, which were isolated from the main compound.

Martyrdom

When the flames reached the armoury it exploded, creating enough confusion among the Germans to allow a number of prisoners to attempt to break out. In the chaos those armed with blunt weapons killed the nearest guard – 20 Germans were killed in this way and their guns taken – while others threw wooden planks and boards into place to bridge the flooded ditches and the wire. But the Germans quickly recovered and picked off the fleeing prisoners with a withering hail of automatic fire. Fewer than 200 of the 700-strong population of Treblinka succeeded in evading capture or being killed by their guards. Of those who escaped, 18 months of hardship and danger and a perilous journey through hostile country lay ahead of them before they were able to stop looking over their shoulders – although none would ever be able to put the past behind them.

In the end, only 12 of the Treblinka escapees lived to see the end of the war.

All of the prisoners knew they had little chance of surviving the break-out, but escape had not been their primary objective. They sacrificed themselves to destroy the camp. As Samuel Rajzman later wrote: 'Our plan of action was worked out entirely in the direction of destroying the camp ... We realized our aim fully and in martyrdom ... A fortress of horrible Nazism was erased from the face of the earth.'

Auschwitz

Auschwitz, the generic name given to the site of the largest complex of Nazi concentration, extermination and slave labour camps in southern Poland (the site comprised three large camps and 45 sub-camps), is synonymous with genocide, a hateful symbol of man's inhumanity and a grim warning of the unspeakable cruelty that can result from racism and extremism.

From March 1942 until its liberation by the Russians in January 1945, it operated as one of Hitler's most efficient death factories, exterminating up to 6,000 people a day with thousands more dying from starvation, disease, torture, punishment beatings and as the result of sadistic medical experiments.

During that time its existence was unknown to all but the Nazi leadership and those who were employed to run the camp and transport its human cargo to their hellish destination. Its location had been chosen both for its remoteness and its accessibility by rail, ensuring that its existence was concealed from the general population.

Despite their later denials, the local inhabitants of Oświęcim (Auschwitz) would have been aware of its function as many had been employed in its construction and lived within sight or smell of the crematorium. But when rumours began to circulate in Germany regarding the conditions in the camps, they were invariably dismissed as anti-Nazi propaganda or as 'horror stories' designed to frighten the population into unquestioning obedience and submission to the regime.

Horror reports disbelieved

The Nazis went to considerable trouble to disguise the true purpose of these *Konzentrationslager*, or concentration camps. They released only highly selective newsreel footage of their model camp at Theresienstadt, where the healthy-looking inmates were paraded for inspection by the Red Cross and visiting SS officers, including Reichsführer Himmler.

In 1944 the Berlin-born filmmaker Kurt Gerron, a veteran of the First World War, was forced to direct a Nazi propaganda film, for screening in neutral countries, documenting the 'humane' conditions inside Theresienstadt. Immediately after filming was completed, he and his wife were transported to Auschwitz together with the crew where they were all murdered on arrival.

When initial reports of the brutality and the extermination process reached the Allies, they were received with incredulity. It was simply inconceivable that such horrors were taking place in 20th century Europe. It has been said that even those involved in the anti-Nazi resistance movement in Europe and who 'were familiar with the endless cruelties of the Nazis' did not believe that the regime was carrying out the systematic murder of millions on an industrial scale.

It therefore fell to the prisoners themselves to provide incontestable proof of the conditions inside Auschwitz-Birkenau, in the hope that if the truth were known the Allies would bomb the railway lines and perhaps also the gas chambers.

Photographic proof

The problem was carefully considered by the Auschwitz underground leader, Józef Cyrankiewicz, who was able to continue directing resistance operations in the Cracow ghetto thanks to a network of go-betweens who would smuggle themselves into Auschwitz to receive their orders. Cyrankiewicz advocated secretly photographing the crematorium and the piles of bodies, so that no one would ever be able to deny what had happened. It would be an extremely dangerous assignment, but it was agreed that it was the only possible course of action open to them.

Cyrankiewicz, a future premier of Poland, entrusted the task to fellow Pole David Szmulewski, a tall, dark-haired, physically imposing man described as someone 'who had been at war all his life', although he was then only 30. In the early 1930s he had made his way to Palestine to escape persecution in his homeland but was expelled by the British for his activities in the Palestine Communist Party. From Palestine he travelled to Spain to join the fight against Franco's fascists and when they crushed the communist International Brigade he fled to France, where he was captured by the Germans. He was first sent to Dachau, then to Sachsenhausen and finally to Auschwitz.

Secret camera

Szmulewski had been one of the first to volunteer to help with the construction of the prisoners' quarters, although he did not have the skills he claimed to possess. But he knew that his best chance of survival lay in giving the impression that he could be useful to his jailers.

Later, his work was to prove extremely useful to the underground as he was allowed to move freely around the camp unguarded. The underground infiltrated every facility in the camp including the *Effectenkammer*, the 35 huge warehouses where the personal belongings of recent arrivals were stored until they could be sorted and shipped back to Germany.

Among the abandoned items were countless numbers of cameras, so Szmulewski only had to ask a contact to pocket one small enough to be easily concealed. The underground even had men in the Sonderkommando, the work detail which operated the four crematoria and the open pits where bodies were burned and whose duties were terminated whenever their German overseers felt it was time to replace them. Life expectancy for a Sonderkommando could be anything from a few weeks to three months, but even that was considerably more than the average inmate could expect. For this reason, they were prepared to risk their lives aiding the underground.

Sneaked pictures

Once the plan to obtain the photographs had been approved one of the crematorium detail deliberately damaged the roof, so that a roofer would be required to fix it. Szmulewski would be sent to do the job, but as he would be subjected to a routine search the camera would have to be smuggled in by hiding it in the false bottom of a large kettle used to carry soup from the kitchen to the Sonderkommando.

With the preparations completed, Szmulewski left for what was supposedly a routine repair. For what seemed like hours, he waited until the Oberscharführer (senior squad leader) left the compound to supervise the arrival of another transport so he could retrieve the camera without being seen. He tucked it beneath his jacket with the lens poking through an enlarged buttonhole and had just enough time to take three pictures. The first was of a group of naked women being herded towards the gas chambers and the other two were of the burning pits, or 'roasts' as the Germans called them.

There was no need to keep the camera, so he removed the film, wrapped it in a rag and covered it with the tar he had brought in a bucket to repair the roof. Then he hid the camera and returned to his block with the precious evidence. Once the film was retrieved it was smuggled out to the Cracow underground with a report by Cyrankiewicz detailing the scale of the atrocities, which he described as having 'no parallel in history' and 'vast in scope and bestial in execution'. He continued:

'Transports of Hungarian Jews have been arriving here in quick succession since the middle of May 1944, eight transports a night and five a day, night after night and day after day, each train of forty-eight to fifty wagons, with one hundred people in each wagon … Both gas chambers are working without interruption, yet they cannot catch up. Only enough time is allowed between the gassing of one group and the admission of another, to air the room … The four crematoria smoke incessantly and so do the pyres under the open sky.'

Incredibly, despite now having the photographic evidence and an eyewitness account of what was taking place in Auschwitz, the Allies refused to mount a bombing raid on the Polish railway line in the region or on the complex itself. But more than 70 years later, those three photographs prove the lie to those who would deny the Holocaust.

Abandoned to their fate

By October 1944 the Auschwitz underground had resigned themselves to the fact that there would be no Allied air-raids and that all their efforts to convince the outside world of the urgency to intervene had been in vain. The transports continued to arrive day and night, bringing tens of thousands of defenceless victims to the gas chambers, which operated continuously seven days a week.

The prisoners would now have to take matters into their own hands. But they knew that they would not survive any attempt to destroy the gas chambers.

In the death camps, women were as willing to sacrifice their lives as the men, if it meant putting an end to, or even only disrupting, the exterminations.

Rosa Robota, 23, was working in the *Bekleidungstelle* (clothing unit) when she was approached by a member of the Auschwitz underground who needed her help in contacting the women in the Krupp-owned munitions factory. It was one of many industrial plants within the camp manned by slave labour, who were working in shifts to maintain production 24 hours a day.

Male prisoners were prohibited from talking to the plant's female workers, but Rosa would be able to contact them without

Prisoners' shoes from Treblinka: a poignant reminder that the Nazis' 'industrialization of death' in the Holocaust involved countless individual victims.

arousing suspicion and she knew a few of the women from the Ciechanów ghetto from where she and her family had been transported in November 1942.

Revolt begins too soon

Rosa soon recruited 20 women, who began smuggling out button-sized slivers of dynamite. These were handed over to a Russian prisoner, who constructed the bombs using sardine tins. Male prisoners working in the munitions factory added to the stock of dynamite by concealing their explosive discs in the false bottom of a soup canister.

Had they had more time to accumulate enough explosive they hoped to blow up the gas chambers and the crematorium and stage a break-out in the ensuing confusion.

But on 17 October 1944, before the preparations for a co-ordinated revolt could be finalized, the Sonderkommando in Birkenau (Auschwitz II) learned that they were next in line for the gas chambers. They could keep silent and go to their deaths hoping that their silence might buy time for the revolt, or they could act now and in their martyrdom take some of the hated Germans with them.

They chose to detonate their bombs and destroy one of the four crematoria. Several guards were wounded in the hand to hand fighting that followed, while four SS men were killed and a fifth guard was pushed into an oven. Of the 140,000 prisoners at Auschwitz-Birkenau, an estimated 600 managed to follow the surviving Sonderkommando through the gap they had cut in the barbed wire. But it is believed that every one of them was killed by SS units who were sent out in pursuit.

Silent under torture

In the aftermath, Rosa and three of her female accomplices were arrested and tortured by the SS. Every day two female guards dragged her from the condemned cell to the interrogation block, where she was beaten until her face had swollen and her hair was matted with dried blood. Her comrades knew that she would not betray them and they wanted her to know that she was not alone in her suffering. So one night they plied a guard in the condemned block with liquor and took his keys. One of them slipped into Rosa's cell and found her sprawled on the bare concrete floor. She was barely recognizable. With the cries and moans of the other inmates echoing around the unlit corridors, he strained to hear her last words, which described the tortures she had endured and her assurance that despite all that she had suffered she had not betrayed her friends. She had given her interrogators only one name, that of a Sonderkommando she knew had died in the break-out. She was prepared to die and would accept her fate if she could be sure that her comrades were continuing the struggle. He promised her that they were and then he left.

Four days later Rosa and her three female accomplices were publicly hanged in the Appelplatz, where the prisoners were assembled for roll call.

The destruction of the crematorium shook up the

commandant, who increased the number of sentries posted around the perimeter and maintained the outer cordon night and day. Routine searches were intensified and thousands of Poles were transferred to other camps in the belief that they had been the primary architects of the revolt and would be capable of instigating another. The three undamaged gas chambers continued to function, but the Germans had seen what the Jews were capable of when they were faced with annihilation and they never again underestimated the potential threat they posed to their 'New Order'.

But in the words of Yehuda Bauer, Czech-born Holocaust historian:

'The horror of the Holocaust is not that it deviated from human norms; the horror is that it didn't. What happened may happen again to others, not necessarily Jews, perpetrated by others, not necessarily Germans. We are all possible victims, possible perpetrators, possible bystanders.'

Bibliography

Ainsztein, Reuben *Jewish Resistance in Nazi-Occupied Eastern Europe* (Elek 1974)

Mark, Bernard 'The Warsaw Ghetto Uprising', in Yuri Suhl (ed.) *They Fought Back* (Paperback Library 1968)

Daimant, David *Héros Juifs de la Résistance Française* (Verlag 1964)

Dworzecki, Mark *The Jerusalem of Lithuania in Struggle and Destruction* (Mapai Press 1951)

Eckman, Lester and Lazar, Chaim *The Jewish Resistance* (Shengold 1977)

Goeschel, Christian *Suicide in Nazi Germany* (Oxford University Press 2009)

Grynberg, Michael (ed.) *Words to Outlive Us* (Granta 2003)

Gutman, Israel *Resistance* (Mariner Books 1994)

Lanski, Mordekhai Yad Vashem Document Archive, O.33/257, manuscript, pp. 306–307

Lewin, Abraham *A Cup of Tears* (Fontana 1990)

Moczarski, Kazimierz *Conversations with an Executioner* (Prentice Hall 1981)

Neiberg, Arieh *The Last Ones* (publisher unknown)

Olenski, Luba *A Life Reclaimed* (Makor Jewish Community Library 2006)

Ringelblum, Emanuel *Notes from the Warsaw Ghetto* ed. Jacob Solan (Schoken 1958)

Smolar, Hersh *Resistance in Minsk* (Oakland 1966)

Solan, Jacob (ed.) *Notes from the Warsaw Ghetto* (Schoken 1958)

Suhl, Yuri (ed.) *They Fought Back* (Schoken 1975)

Tec, Nechama *Defiance* (Oxford 1993)

Vrba, Rudolph and Bestic, Alan *I Cannot Forgive* (Bantam 1964)

Werner, Harold *Fighting Back* (Columbia University Press 1992)

Resources

www.aish.com

www.en.wikipedia.org

www.humanityinaction.org

www.jewishvirtuallibrary.org

www.stcatherinesstandard.ca

www.telegraph.co.uk

www.theage.com.au

www.yadvashem.org

www.ynetnews.com

Periodicals

Ainsztein, Reuben 'The Bialystok Ghetto Revolt' (*Jewish Quarterly*, London 1956)

Koniuchowski, Leyb 'The Revolt of the Jews of Marcinkonis' (*YIVO Annual of Jewish Social Science* 1953)

Zukerman, William 'The Revolt in the Ghetto' (*Harper's Magazine*, September 1943)

Index

Picture credits

Getty Images: 15, 18, 27, 33, 52, 57,63, 75, 113, 121, 126, 133, 143, 147, 164, 179

United States Holocaust Memorial Museum: 83

Otto Weidt Museum: 41

Wiki: 66, 136

PikiWiki_Israel: 85